How I Made Six Figures *in* One Month

$100,000

by
STEVEN LINTON

BIG AIR PUBLISHING
SCOTTSDALE, ARIZONA

Published by Big Air Publishing
14795 N. 78th Way, Ste. 1000
Scottsdale, AZ 85260

Publisher's Cataloging-in-Publication Data
Linton, Steven.

How I made six figures in one month / by Steven Linton – Scottsdale,
AZ : Big Air Pub., 2006.

p. ; cm.
ISBN: 0-9773304-0-0
ISBN13: 978-0-9773304-0-9

1. Multilevel marketing. 2. Success. 3. Success in business I. Title.

HF5415.126 .L56 2005
658.8/72-dc22   2005934393

Book production and coordination by Jenkins Group, Inc.
www.bookpublishing.com
Interior design by Cecile Kaufman
Cover design by Jim Weems

Printed in the United States of America
10 09 08 07 06 · 5 4 3 2 1

To order additional copies of this book call
1-800-247-6553

Contents

ACKNOWLEDGMENTS

In May of 1995, I left college with my master's degree in aviation safety, expecting that flying would be my livelihood for the rest of my working years. It's funny how things can change. I am not disappointed that I did not stay in flying, though I did always want to fly the Boeing 737. My only regret is that my mother and father are not here to share my life.

My father did not have a lot of faith in anything that was not a "real" job, and I am sure he would be astonished to see that life does exist outside the box. I also know Dad would be proud to see the journey I have taken to get to where I am. He also would have smiled to see me fly Citation Jets, Lear-25's, and for FedEx.

My mother, unfortunately, missed everything in my life past the age of thirteen. Nonetheless, she has been my inspiration since I first found my entrepreneurial spirit ten years ago, for she was very successful in network marketing long before I knew what network marketing was.

My mother and father are a huge part of my life even today, long after they both have gone. I would like to thank them from the deepest part of my heart for all they have done for me through life and through spirit. I love them both very much!

To Lori and Sarah, I would like to say thank you for not giving up on me over the years. It has not always been easy, but I'm glad we have grown close again. Lori, you have given me inspiration when it has been missing in my life. From the time you were eighteen years old, you have gone out and set the world on fire. Your work ethic is unmatched and your spirit is truly uplifting. Thank you for being the most wonderful sister on earth.

Sarah, I am so proud of you and all you have done in your young life. I look forward to watching and sharing your incredible achievements as you grow up. You have made me very proud. Thank you both so much for being supportive and for not judging me for taking the road less traveled. I love you both.

Several years ago, I was flipping through the classified ads of the local paper looking for a day job while I was flying for FedEx at night. I saw an ad that said "Work from home . . ." Not realizing the ad was for a network marketing opportunity, which at the time I knew nothing about, I called the ad and spoke with a gentleman who was selling something I did not have any interest in. For some reason we seemed to bond, and although I did not get involved with his opportunity, we stayed in touch through phone calls every month or so just to say hello and talk about flying and skydiving.

A couple of years later, I decided to leave my flying career and I called him up to ask if he would share his opportunity with me. That day was the beginning of one of the most incredible journeys a person could ever experience, not to mention an incredible friendship. I have learned so much from this person, and although we have been out of touch lately, I still have incredible respect and love for him. He has shown me what is truly possible in my life, and for that I will always be grateful. For everything we have shared, learned, and achieved, together and apart, I love you, Brent. I respect you, I thank you, and I miss you.

There are so many people who deserve to be recognized for their part in my achievements, but the space available will not permit me to list them all. I would nevertheless like to give a heartfelt thanks to a few of the people who have been inspirational and who hold a special place in my heart. My warmest wishes and thanks go out to Pattie Lewis, my life-long best friend Bruce Morris, Julia Payne, Shane and Michelle Krider, Lisa and Bobby Molina, Jay and Tammy McNeil, Dawn Henderson, Mark and Brandi Bauer, Bob Proctor, Tom Hopkins, and Ron Marks. You are all inspirational. May our paths someday cross again.

If it were not for the love, friendship, support, and mentorship of all these people over the past ten years, I do not believe I would be on the path I am on today. I love you and thank you all.

INTRODUCTION

Hello, my name is Steve Linton. The book you are about to read started out as a training manual for a network marketing company where I was an associate several years ago. I originally wrote the book as a tool to help associates get their businesses off the ground and making money as quickly as possible.

The information contained within these pages is drawn from my first-hand experience of what it took to generate over $100,000 profit in one month. There is no secret ingredient to being successful in network marketing. It simply requires that you be clear about what you want to achieve and that you be committed. The most important thing to remember is, *never quit.*

My career in network marketing originally began in 1996. Like many people, I responded to a simple newspaper ad that said something about making money from home. At the time, I was a pilot for a major overnight freight airline and was looking to supplement my income.

After responding to the ad, I quickly found myself engulfed in a whole new world. This new world and the people in it were different from anything I had experienced previously. The people were mostly upbeat and positive, and I liked that, since I was not very happy or positive at that time. Most of the people I came into contact with had great energy and were willing to help me see my true potential, which was something I had never thought about before. "My true potential . . . ?"

It had never dawned on me to consider what was actually possible in my life, but the more time I spent with these people, the more their energy rubbed off on and affected me. As I began to embrace the concepts of personal development and put them to use in my life, I began to see incredible changes taking place each day.

I went on to become the top income earner for my first year with that company, as well as to set an income record that stood for some time. The principles and practices that helped me create such results are outlined in detail within this book. If you are currently an associate or an affiliate with a network marketing company, this book will share all of these practices along with other helpful tips and ideas that will lead you and your business to the next level.

If you are not associated with a network marketing company but are considering becoming an affiliate, this book will give you a jump-start and will dramatically reduce your learning curve, which is where many people who begin in network marketing unfortunately remain.

This business is a learning process, but many people who come into network marketing have the idea that it is easy and that someone will be there to do the work for them. They think that just because they enroll with a company and put some money into it, they will automatically have success.

Nothing could be further from the truth. Understand this: regardless of what company you decide to go with, they all require work, and no one is going to do it for you. If you have the desire and are trainable and willing to learn, success in this business is quite simple, but that in no way means it is easy.

In this book, I will show you how I was able to generate over $30,000 a day and over $100,000 in a month – *profit*. This book will walk you step-by-step through starting and building a successful network marketing business. At the back of the book, you will find an appendix that has several resources which will also help you as you are building your business. Again, there is no magic formula or secret ingredient to being successful. If you use the information in this book, and I mean *really* use it, you can experience the same success and more.

May you have all the success in the world.

You truly deserve it!

Begin with the End

Before I begin, I would like to define just what a network marketing company is, along with how and why a person becomes associated with one. Network marketing is somewhat of a generic term for a business that is based on building a team of associates or distributors who work together to market or sell a product or service. Each associate or distributor, who is a representative of the company, works independently from the other associates. However, each associate benefits financially from the team he or she builds. When an associate builds a team of distributors, the associate earns a percentage of the profit or revenue from each and every distributor who becomes a part of that associate's team, forever.

As an independent representative of a network marketing company, a person is not an employee of the company and does not "hire" distributors for their own organization. When new distributors (another name for independent representatives of the company) enroll or begin working with a network marketing company, they generally enroll or sign up with an existing associate. Even though they have signed up with an existing associate, these people are not employees; they are considered to be self-employed. Depending on the company and its compensation plan, associates may receive their commissions through a check from the company, and in that case they receive a form 1099 (independent contractor form) from the company.

There are many types of network marketing companies as well as many different types of compensation plans. As the industry has grown over the years, some companies have attempted to conduct business unethically by offering compensation plans with no products or services. Unfortunately, the network marketing industry now has an unfair negative stigma attached to it due to these unethical companies.

Network marketing and the many different compensation plans can be divided into two categories, multi-level and not multi-level. "Multi-level" is a compensation plan that pays associates a commission on their own sales as well as a percentage of everyone's sales within their team. This is an extremely powerful way to build a business.

On the other side of the coin is the non-multi-level compensation plan. An example of this would be the Australian two-up plan. With this compensation structure, you simply pass the first two sales you make up to your advisor/director/sponsor, after which time you do not share your commissions with anyone, ever. This creates a very level playing field for all the associates in the company.

Generally, a company that uses this compensation structure will refer to these two sales as "training sales." The new associate passes the first two sales up in exchange for the training received from the sponsor. Once associates have passed up their training sales to their sponsors, they have the ability to generate more money than anyone in the company, regardless of how long they have been in the company.

This situation is not likely to occur in a multi-level compensation plan due to the fact that in multi-level there is generally a residual component to the compensation plan that builds and grows over time. After five or ten years, the residual income in a multi-level structure will be tough to overcome by someone just coming into the business.

The Australian two-up plan is powerful in its own regard due to the fact that once you are qualified as an advisor or director, meaning that you have passed up your first two training sales, you not only have the ability to be the top income earner for the month on your very first month, but anyone you bring into your business must pass up their first two training sales to you before they can start generating their own commissions.

In that case, if you brought in ten new distributors your first month, each one of them would have to pass up their first two training sales directly to you in order for each of them to start generating income of their own. That equates to twenty additional sales, over the original ten, that all go directly to you. Depending on the amount of commission that an associate retains from the sale of their product or service, this can be a substantial amount of money.

The draw to the network marketing industry is becoming stronger every day. The industrial age is gone; welcome to the information age. Today, the old-school thinking of "Go to a good school and get a good job, work hard, and retire on a strong retirement plan" is being replaced with a more productive and progressive mindset: "Work hard for yourself instead of someone else so you can retire wealthy instead of them retiring early and wealthy and you retiring late and broke."

People are realizing there are better ways to provide for themselves and their families than by punching a clock for $35,000 a year. The "rat race" is alive and well, and more and more people are not only realizing they are in it, they are looking for a way out of it. Network marketing is now being recognized as one of the best ways out of the rat race. Many of the corporate sales trainers as well as the personal development trainers headlining the huge seminars today have come from or participated in network marketing opportunities.

Another reason network marketing is becoming more accepted is the flexibility people have when working in a networking opportunity. It is not necessary to live in a major metropolitan area in order to have success. A person can live virtually anywhere as long as they have a few basic essentials such as a phone and possibly a fax and computer. Most network marketing opportunities are designed so that associates can market their business to opportunity seekers all over the world.

Even with all of the advantages to starting and building a network marketing business, the fact is that many people shy away from anything that is home-based because they have been conditioned by industrial-age thinkers to believe that all home-based businesses are scams. I know this because I used to be one of them. Once I learned to open my mind to the fact that there are no absolutes, I found that I could create literally anything I wanted for myself. I encourage you to do the same.

Okay, you are a new associate. Now what?

As a former professional pilot and an all-around aviation nut, I have a love for just about everything that flies, falls, or jumps through the air. You will see quickly that I use references to flying and skydiving often to illustrate my points. There are many parallels between flying, skydiving, and the lessons in this book. It is not required that you enjoy flying or jumping out of airplanes to benefit from this information, but if you will let your imagination take you there, I can help you have the same emotional impact, which is one of the ways to effect a change in yourself.

My goal for this book is not only to help you have more success in your business, whether it is a network marketing business or otherwise, but also to assist you in having more success in all areas of your life and to recognize your true potential. I would like for you to see that the only limitations you have in business or in life are the ones you place on yourself. In order to do that, we will want to look at three areas of your life: where you arc currently, where you want to go, and how you plan to get there.

This whole process of transforming your life and your business is a lot like filing a flight plan. As a pilot, before I take off on a long trip, I generally file a flight plan. A flight plan helps me see not only where I am currently and where I am going, it also helps me see how I will get there. These three areas are referred to as the departure point, destination, and route of flight.

Where do you start? Before I answer, take a minute and figure out where you are now. Before you can get to where you are going, it is helpful to know where you are. I call this the "departure point." When you are determining your departure point, it is extremely important to be as authentic as you possibly can. Sometimes this is difficult, especially if you have not achieved all you have set out to achieve by this point in your life. Just remember, the most important thing is to be honest with yourself and to recognize where you are, good or bad.

If you were taking a trip in your car, you wouldn't just jump in the car and start driving, would you? The same is true here, which is why I strongly recommend beginning with the end result you desire and working backwards. You must know exactly where you want to end up on your journey before you can determine the best route to get there. The end result is what I refer to as the "destination." When you are considering your destination, ask yourself some questions before you finalize any decisions about your destination. First, ask yourself, "What do I want?"

The best way to answer that question is to put yourself in a quiet, comfortable environment such as a quiet room in your house or office, with no distractions from kids, TV's, radios, telephones, or pets. Once you have gotten yourself in such an environment, close your eyes and imagine yourself in the future. See yourself one year, five years, ten years, and twenty-five years in the future. Now, what will your life be like? What will you have accomplished in that much time? What will you have accumulated in your life as far as assets, property, and relationships go? How many people will you have helped? Remember, you are the creator, the architect, of your own reality. You can create anything you desire, so don't hold back. Make your reality exactly what you want it to be.

As you see yourself during this process, it is imperative that you not judge or second-guess yourself. Do not question whether such a life is possible. If you can see it in your mind, it *is* possible. Just see yourself the way you will be at that time in your life. If you see yourself as the top income earner in your company, great! If you see yourself as the CEO of your own company with a thousand employees and offices in seven countries, that's great, too.

A key to getting the most out of this visualization technique is, first, to use all your senses as you visualize. When you see yourself in the future, pay attention to the details. How do you look? What is your hairstyle? How do you dress? What kind of clothes or suits do you wear? Look at your shoes – do they shine or are they flip-flops? Are you wearing jewelry? How do you walk? Do you have good posture? What do you sound like when you speak? How do people respond to you in group settings? What do you drive? Where do you live? How big is your home? What kind of philanthropic work do you do?

Because all results begin as thoughts, it is important that you not leave out any of these details when you visualize. What you leave out here will also be left out of your reality in the future.

Most importantly, when you go through this process and see yourself as you will be in the future, make sure that who you are and what you do is bigger than yourself. *What you do must serve others.* Remember, the surest way to get what you want in life is to help others get what they want. This is one of the laws of the universe. *What you sow, so shall you reap.* If you make your life about giving and helping others, you will never have a problem receiving.

CHAPTER 1 SUMMARY

$\mathcal{N}$etwork marketing describes a business that is based on building a team of associates or distributors who work together to market or sell a product or service. Network marketing is quickly becoming the expressway out of the "rat race" because people can live virtually anywhere and build their business as long as they have a few basic essentials such as a phone and possibly a fax and computer. When building a network marketing business, begin with a few key points in mind:

Your end result must be clearly defined. It is not enough to say, "I want a new home." Your goal must be specific. What kind of home do you want? How big is it? Where is it located? What kind of floor plan does it have? Is it a custom home? How many rooms does it have? What does the inside look like? How many windows does it have? Is it on a large piece of property or in a neighborhood? When you define exactly what your goal is, visit the image or the real thing as often as you can. Touch it. Feel it. Smell it. Use all of your senses to take mental ownership of the object of your goal.

File *your flight plan*. Know your departure point, your destination, and your route of flight.

Define where you are. How can you get where you want to go if you do not know where you are? Establish where you want to want to go. What do you want?

Create your end result through visualization and study it every day. Your subconscious mind will soon manifest it into physical form.

Determine the route you will take to reach the destination. Develop discipline in your daily routine so that you always make time for visualization exercises. Finally, make sure you help others along the way.

Remember that your goals must be bigger than you. The surest way to get what you want in life is to help others get what they want. This is a law of the universe. What you sow, so shall you reap. Regardless of what you do in life, whatever you put out into the universe, the universe will give back to you tenfold.

CHAPTER *2*

What Is Personal Development?

Before we get into the details of how to generate six figures in one month, I would like to cover some information that I believe is the foundation of any true success. Success starts in the subconscious mind before anything is ever manifested into reality. In order to experience success in any part of your life, you must practice personal development in some form.

I understand that the concept of personal development is foreign to most people. Many people believe that the results they get in life are just "what they get" and that they can't do a thing about it. The fact is, you have the ability to create any result you want in life. You can be, do, and have anything you desire, as long as you understand the concepts of this thing called personal development.

Personal development means learning to change the way you think about your life and all that is part of your life. We all grow up with certain beliefs and convictions about things such as politics, religion, sex, relationships, and just about everything else. Personal development means being able to step aside from these beliefs and convictions and consider the possibility that some of them are not a part of you. In fact, most of your beliefs have probably been handed to you by your parents or peers without you even knowing it.

What does that mean to you? If your beliefs and convictions are not a part of you, meaning they did not originally come from you, then they came from somewhere else. That means you may be living your life according to someone else's beliefs.

For example, let's say you believe that in order to get ahead in life, you must go to college and earn a degree. You must then get a good job with a solid company, and if you want to make more money, you must get a better job.

Is that true? It can be, but it is not a part of any success formula. However, most people will say "Yes" to that question because that is how they have been conditioned.

The fact is, our society has crammed this type of thinking into our heads for so long that most people don't question it and indeed follow it blindly.

Let's take a look at it from another perspective. If you asked this same question of the twenty-one-year-old son of a multi-millionaire, do you think he would tell you that the way to get ahead is to "get a good job"?

Chances are, no, because millionaires think differently and subsequently raise their children to have a different belief system than someone who makes an average income, which is about $30,000 to $50,000 a year in the United States. Such individuals simply are not going to see the way to get ahead as working for someone else.

Let me ask you a question: how many multi-millionaires have you heard of who made their fortune working for someone else? I don't know of one. Please understand, I am not suggesting there is anything wrong with working for someone else if that is what works for you. I just do not believe this is the best way to pursue any substantial amount of wealth.

Personal development means being able to look at this example and consider that the way you view it is not necessarily what's right or the way that everybody views it. The point is to get you to open your mind to the fact that you can be, do, and have anything you want in life. All you have to do is learn to change the way you think.

For example, if you were given the task of cleaning out all the dirty water from the inside of a jar that was affixed to a countertop and you could not pick up the jar to pour out the dirty water, what would you do? You could take a large container of clean water and pour it into the jar of dirty water until eventually all the dirty water flowed out and you were left with only clean water.

This is essentially what we can do with our subconscious minds. The way we do this is by replacing limiting beliefs and negative thoughts with a new belief system and self-image. This can be accomplished through affirmations, visualizations, and goal setting as well as other techniques that work through repetition.

As we go through this section, we will look mostly at how personal development can assist you in achieving your business goals and how your results can and will carry over into other areas of your life. We will also look at the other areas of your life that have nothing to do with this business, thereby opening up a whole new world of possibilities for yourself. So, let's get started.

FEAR

I am going to begin this section with FEAR, an acronym that stands for "False Expectations Appearing Real." The reason I am starting with FEAR is that, in my opinion, FEAR is the number one thing that holds people in mediocrity. It must be addressed before anything else can be accomplished.

Being an associate with a network marketing company, whether you are brand new or a seasoned veteran, requires some ability to get "out of the box." You will not be able to sufficiently get "out of the box" until you address your FEARs. The whole purpose of this section is to help you do just that.

First, I would like to talk about where FEARs come from. Most FEARs come from a lack of information or education about what is FEARed. I'm not going to analyze your nightmares or anything; I simply want to focus on the real life FEARs that hold you back from higher levels of success. I would like you to think of something in your mind that brings FEAR to you. Now, I want you to ask yourself a question: how much do you really know about that source? Please be honest. Do you know a lot or a little?

Let's talk about flying. Many people are afraid to fly. You may not be, but many people are. If you talk to someone on an airplane about why they are afraid to fly, you will generally get the same answer. I know this because I have been a pilot for almost twenty years and I have asked hundreds of people this very question. Most people will tell you they are afraid the plane will crash. I know that sounds like an obvious answer, but when I ask the next question, "Why are you afraid the plane will crash?" I get the same answer most of the time. They tell me they are afraid the plane might fall out of the sky or crash into another plane.

When I first started my flight training, I remember taking off in a Cessna 152 and feeling that flinch of my body each time the plane hit a bump or rocked to the side. When it happened, I wanted to brace myself against the sides of the plane as if the plane were going to stop flying. This is a natural reaction when your subconscious mind has not been conditioned to know that the plane works by the strict laws of physics and, under normal circumstances, will not fall out of the sky.

The air traffic control system in the United States is also not widely understood by the general public. The fact is, the system that allows airplanes to fly without crashing into each other is very precise. Accidents happen, but flying is usually very safe, and most FEARs of flying come from a lack of information or education about the subject.

I would like you to try a visualization exercise. I understand that you are reading and probably cannot read with your eyes closed, so I would like you to allow yourself to really be a part of the story. I want you to be the person I am talking about. As I take you through this experience, I will be acting as if I am talking directly to you. I want you to be the person

I am talking with and respond to me in your mind just as you would if we were actually in conversation. The more you allow yourself to be present in this experience, the more you will get out of it.

I am now speaking to you, and I will leave a blank like this _____ every time I say your name. This is more effective than you seeing a name that is not yours. Remember, _____ , when you see a blank, say your name in your head, because I am talking to you. Are you ready, _____? Great! Let's go.

One of my favorite things to do is surprise people for their birthdays. I can't remember when your birthday is and I'm sure I missed the last one, so I'm going to surprise you with a gift today. I will be over to your house to pick you up in ten minutes, so be ready.

I know that was a short ten minutes, _____ , but are you ready to go? Good. We can take my car, so let's get going. It will be about a thirty-minute drive to where we are going for your surprise. While we are driving, I would like to share some thoughts with you.

First, I would like you to know that this surprise is <u>not</u> an option. It is already paid for and a refund is not possible. When we get there, _____ , if for any reason you think you might have some FEARs that would keep you from enjoying this surprise, I want you to put them aside and concentrate on the experience.

Okay, _____ , we are almost there. As we pull into the drive, I want you to close your eyes and I'll walk

you to the door. As you get out of the car, watch your step. Hold onto my arm and I'll lead you. Okay, just a few more steps. Now, _____ , I'm going to put you in place here and when I count to three, I want you to open your eyes and see your surprise. Are you ready, _____?
Are you sure? Okay. One, two, three! Open your eyes, _____ , because I'm taking you on a <u>skydive</u>!

Alright, _____ , I know you might have some FEAR about this, but I assure you everything is going to be okay. I've got ten years in the sport and almost 7,000 jumps, so I know you are going to be fine. What we are going to do is go inside and fill out some paperwork and then we will meet with your tandem master who will be taking you on your jump. Don't worry, I'll be right there with you because I'm going to jump with you and capture your entire experience on video so you can show all your friends and family. Are you excited? Great! Let's go.

Now that you have the paperwork done, I want to introduce you to Dean. Dean will be your tandem master today and he is going to make sure that you have a great time and come back safely. Dean, this is _____ , and _____ , this is Dean. Great. Now, _____ , why don't you come over here and put this jumpsuit on—you'll probably have to take your shoes off. While you are doing that, I'm going to get my camera equipment ready.

As I walk away to get my camera, I look back at you and see the emotion taking over. I can see the FEAR starting to set in. You are starting to sweat. When I come back with my camera, you are sitting there waiting and looking at the other people coming in from the landing area. I can almost see the knots building inside your stomach.

Are you ready to head to the plane, _____? We are on a five-minute call, so we are going out to the tram that will take us down to the plane. Now, _____ , as we approach the plane I want you to stay right next to me so I can be sure you don't walk into the prop, okay? I won't be able to talk to you once we get on the plane because we won't be sitting together, so have fun and I'll see you in freefall. Watch your head when you go up the step so you don't smack it on the floater bar. Hey, _____ , remember to have fun. I'm going to be right in front of you during the freefall, so don't forget to smile, and don't get fixated on the ground. Look around and enjoy the view.

I get you up the ladder and onto the plane. You and Dean are sitting all the way toward the pilot, and I am in the back of the plane by the door. I love this part. I get to capture all the emotion on video and show someone a world they otherwise wouldn't know.

As we taxi out with the engines at a loud roar, I look at your face and see that FEAR is really setting in. I zoom in on you to truly capture the emotion you are experiencing as you stare out the window with a blank look. As the plane climbs through ten thousand feet on the way to fourteen thousand, we are getting closer to my favorite part.

We are about sixty seconds from exiting. I look down the bench at you to get one last close-up and I see tears run-

ning down your face. I know you are scared, but I'm betting it will be totally different when we are back on the ground.

I look up and the yellow light comes on, which means we are about ten seconds from jumping. A skydiver next to me yells "Door!" That lets everyone know the door is coming open. The five-foot wide, roll-up door of the twin Otter jump ship flies open and the rush of cold air fills the cabin. The intensity of the wind noise is sometimes shocking for first-time jumpers.

The group ahead of me positions themselves in the door for exit. The team's captain hollers, "Ready . . . set . . . go!" The four-way team quickly falls away from the back of the door.

It's our turn now. I look down the bench and you and Dean are sliding towards the door. I attempt to establish some quick eye contact with you, but you are fixated on the door. I make one last attempt to communicate with you, and then I lean in close and ask, "Are you ready to skydive?" No answer comes back. Your blank stare looks so familiar. I've seen this look hundreds of times!

I promptly grab the floater bar and swing myself outside the airplane to the camera step. Quickly getting positioned, I look back inside the airplane at you and Dean. Your face is pale and blank. I try to make eye contact, but FEAR is obviously in control right now. Dean begins the exit but is halted by your death-grip on the airplane. Dean struggles to peel your fingers from around the floater bar. Finally, you are ready to go. Dean starts his exit rock . . . ready . . . set . . . go! We all three leave the air-plane. Dean gives you a summersault exit. As you get stable and Dean deploys the drogue, I fly on my back up in front of you and then flip over on my belly. It almost always gets a smile from tandem passengers when they see this body flying upside down in front of them while they are falling at 120 MPH.

I position myself directly in front of and slightly below your face. We are only about ten seconds out of the plane and already your fear has melted away to reveal a grin from ear to ear. The FEAR that was present is now gone and you are looking all around and waving at me. As we fly around the sky, you give me a thumbs-up along with a huge smile.

I film the tandem opening and then hurry down to the landing area so I can film your landing. As you approach overhead, I hear you yelling "Wha-hooo!" You are waving at all the spectators and your laughter is evident. The tandem approaches with a beautiful stand-up landing. Before I can even say a word, you begin yelling, "That was the greatest thing I've ever done – I want to go again!"

I ask, "So, does that mean you enjoyed it?"

You reply by saying, "Oh my God! It was so cool! I didn't feel like I was falling or anything. Watching you fly around was awesome – I didn't know you could fly like that! We were flying!"

This may seem like a silly exercise, but if you let yourself be a part of the story, I'm going to bet you felt some emotions of your own as we got closer to the jump. What is significant about this exercise is the level of FEAR that is present at the beginning versus the end. The reason FEAR is not present at the end is simply that you learn that when you leave the airplane, there is no stomach-in-your-throat feeling, no feeling of falling, the ground does not rush up at you, and you do not die. You realize you can truly fly relative to something else in freefall. All the stuff you created in your head about skydiving is just that – stuff you created! None of it is reality.

The reason you create that stuff is due to a lack of correct information and also because of your conditioning: you are conditioned to believe that if you jump out of an airplane, you will die.

I would like to invite you to take this challenge for real sometime in the future. You will be amazed at what this simple exercise can do for your results as well as your entire life once you get past your FEAR.

LIMITING BELIEFS

Before we get started in this section, I would like to set the record straight on something. You'll find that in addition to flying and skydiving, I make many references to money and use money to illustrate my points quite often. The reason I use money in so many examples is not that I am hung up on money. In fact, I will tell you right now that money will not make you happy. Money is simply a tool. It's a tool that buys freedom, and freedom is what makes people happy. Money is a tool that allows you to extend the good you do for others far beyond the limits of your own physical reach.

The reason I use money in many of my examples is that almost everyone understands money, and just about everyone would like to have more of it. This is where personal development plays a big part in this program. Why is it that most people would like to have more money, but don't?

I'll tell you this: all the money in the world is available to you right now. So why don't you have more of it? Because you've likely been conditioned to believe that, "This is all I can do and I must accept it." Or, "My parents said successful people go to college and get a good-paying job, so that's what I'm going to do."

The people who live by limiting beliefs will not accept that it's possible to make $100,000 to $200,000 or a million dollars per year working for themselves. Why? Because, again, their parents and peers provide the limiting belief system that shapes their world.

Consider this: nowhere in our educational system is there a class called "Becoming Wealthy-101." Our educational system teaches that we should go to college and get a good job, work hard, and get a pension.

Is this the system the wealthy use? Please don't misunderstand me; I'm not saying there is anything wrong with going to college. I have a bachelor's degree and a master's degree myself. What I am attempting to illustrate is that if you want certain things in your life and they're not showing up the way you would like them to, perhaps you need to open your mind to a new way of thinking. When you hear something that is difficult to believe or even comprehend, consider the possibility that it's only because your level of awareness has not reached the proper stage yet.

I'll give you an example: controlled, powered flight seemed impossible until Orville Wright took off on December 17, 1903. Does that mean the Wright brothers invented flying? No. The way to fly an airplane had always existed. It was the Wright brothers who learned how to arrange things in the proper order for the plane to actually fly. All they had to do to accomplish this was raise their level of awareness to discover *how* it could be done. In case you don't already know this, please understand that all the knowledge that ever was or ever will be is present right here and right now and has been since the beginning of time. All we have to do is become aware of it.

When we desire something that seems virtually impossible, all that is required to realize our desires is for us to increase our level of awareness in order to discover how to do it. The next time you catch yourself saying, "I can't do it because . . . " stop, back up, and ask yourself instead, "How can I do it?" Think of it this way: if someone has already done it, then you know it can be done. If what you desire has never been done before, that only means no one has yet discovered how to arrange things in the correct order to accomplish the feat.

Right about now you may be asking yourself what all of this could possibly have to do with making money in network marketing. Well, this is not your ordinary success manual. This book marries personal development to proven marketing techniques that together were the foundation of my success and allowed me to make six figures in one month. When you learn how to open your mind to new possibilities, anything can become achievable.

The masses do not have any idea of what they are truly capable of, both physically and emotionally. Physically, the human body can endure far more than we give it credit for. The same goes for the power of the mind. The reason most people have such limiting beliefs is that they have been programmed by the people around them. In most cases, the people doing the programming are parents and peers. In addition, as we grow and get farther out in the world, we receive new limiting beliefs from our teachers, employers, friends, and our overall environment.

Consider this: in 1954, it was considered impossible to run a mile in under four minutes. The experts agreed that if a person were to run a mile in under four minutes, his or her heart would explode. The four-minute mile was thus deemed an insurmountable human limitation, and the record prior to May 6, 1954, of 4:01.3 had stood for nine years and was considered to be unbreakable.

Roger Bannister, a young medical student, believed otherwise. On May 6, 1954, he broke the four-minute mile with a time of 3:59.4 while fighting a fifteen-mile-per-hour crosswind. Over the next month, three new people broke the four-minute mile, and over the following year more than nineteen people broke the so-called barrier.

Before May 6, 1954, people were conditioned to believe this athletic feat was impossible. Once Roger Bannister proved it could be done, the old conditioning was shattered and many people began to accomplish this athletic feat.

Let me share a personal example. Prior to becoming involved in personal development, I did not believe, nor could I imagine myself, making $100,000 in a year. As I began to have success, my belief system changed. The first time I made $30,000 in a month, I realized I could make $50,000 in a month. As I closed in on my first $50,000-month, I expanded my belief system and knew that I could achieve $100,000 in a month.

Starting out, I didn't believe I could make $100,000 in a year and I found out that I could do it in a month. See, everything is relative. That's a big change in a belief system, and it's a perfect example of how limiting beliefs work. You have the power to create anything you desire for yourself whether you realize it or not. It's simply a matter of increasing your level of awareness in order to become conscious of it.

I like to use the example of Bill Gates walking down the street and coming upon a pile of money. This example will illustrate how everything is relative to your belief system. I've heard it said that if Bill Gates were walking down the street and came across a million dollars in a pile that blocked his path, it would not be worth his time to bend over to pick it up. He makes far more than a million dollars in the time it would take him to pick it all up.

What do you think Bill Gates would say if you told him it was impossible to make $100,000, $500,000, or a million dollars a year working for yourself? Would he agree? No, obviously he would not, because he has a different belief system than most people.

The Law

In order to better understand the concepts I discuss in this section, it will be helpful to have some familiarity with the laws of the universe. There is really only one law: "Energy is." This law has seven subsidiary laws, but for the purposes of this section, I will stick to just a few of the laws that have a direct impact on you and your results.

The law "Energy is" may sound somewhat incomplete to you. You may be asking yourself ". . . is what? What is energy?"

The easiest way to answer this is to say that energy is everything and it is nothing. I'll use an example of the room I am presently in while I write. I can say this is a big room or I can say this is a small room. The truth is that the room is neither big nor small. The room just is. Something cannot be big or small until we compare it to something else. Energy cannot be big or small, good or bad, hot or cold. Energy just is. Everything is only big or small relative to something else. If there were nothing to compare it to, it would just be.

The reason this is important is that your life is affected every day by the laws of the universe, whether you like it or not. If you want to create the best life you can possibly have, you must understand why things happen the way they do. In life, nothing happens by chance or coincidence. Everything happens by law, and understanding the laws by which life happens will elevate your level of awareness, thus allowing you to realize more success in your life. Again, all of the success and all of the knowledge that ever was and ever will be is already here. All you have to do is become aware of it.

THE POWER OF THOUGHT

Think for a moment about all the incredible advancements in technology that have taken place since you were young. Computers, automobiles, airplanes, space travel to other planets—what do they all have in common? They all started as a thought in someone's mind. All things begin as thoughts, which make our thoughts one of the most powerful forms of energy in the universe. If all things begin as thoughts, wouldn't it make sense that if we can hold a thought in our heads, we can manifest that thought into physical form?

I know what you're going to say now: "What if my thought is to fly to the moon?" The great thing about your mind is that it has a built-in governor that keeps us from desiring to achieve more than we are physically capable of achieving. If you are an aspiring artist and your thoughts are primarily directed towards achievements in art, you will not seriously have the desire to run a mile in less than four minutes.

Have you ever found yourself thinking about someone, say a past friend or loved one whom you haven't spoken with in a long time, and within a short time that person just happens to call you on the phone or you run into him or her at the grocery store? Most people chalk that up to coincidence, but this is an example of attracting someone into your life through transfer of thought energy. The fact is, there is remarkable power in thought energy. Your thought energy can range in frequency from very high to very low. A positive thought is on a much higher frequency than a negative thought. Since all energy exists at a particular frequency, your thoughts attract whatever is on the same frequency.

You can actually attract people into your life just like you can attract other results. This is a great way to keep yourself and your energy in check. If you should happen to notice that all of the people around you are incredibly negative, guess what? You are attracting those people into your life because that is the energy you are putting out into the universe. On the other hand, if you see everyone around you as positive and full of great energy, you can bet that you are attracting those people by the same law.

Knowing the awesome power your thoughts have, don't you think it would be a good idea to carefully monitor the thoughts and information you put into your head? It's truly staggering to me how many people begin their day by turning on the TV first thing in the morning and listening to or watching the news. What do you hear when you listen to the news? I know that when I hear a news story, it's almost always negative. It is usually how many people were murdered overnight or car accidents, fires, political corruption, a stock market crash, or war. Why is that? Because negativity sells.

Whether it is a TV news station, magazine, radio station, or a newspaper doesn't matter. Death and destruction sell more than positive stories. If you don't believe that, just look at daytime TV. Have you ever seen anything positive on *Jerry Springer*? With the exception of *Oprah*, you probably will not see anything positive and uplifting on those types of shows because the positive stories typically don't get the ratings.

The question is, why would you want to fill your head with all that negative junk that does nothing except spawn more negative junk in your life? Whatever you put in your mind and give energy to will begin to manifest into your life in a physical form. If you want to achieve more positive results, you must put positive stuff in your head and give positive energy to it.

I have been on a media fast for several years now. When I began to see the power of personal development in my life, I was introduced to the concept of a media fast. This simply means cutting yourself off from all media. That means no TV, radio, newspapers, magazines, or anything except positive and uplifting information such as personal growth books and tapes and music.

I would like to challenge you to a media fast. For the next thirty days, do not read any newspapers or watch any TV or listen to the radio. Take the time you would normally give to these things and use it to read a book or listen to a tape or CD by a personal development author. I'm going to bet you'll feel much better without all the negative junk you normally listen to.

I'm sure some of you are thinking that there is no way you could go for a month without watching TV. Well, guess what? Life existed before TV and newspapers. What does that mean? It means those are learned behaviors that can be unlearned.

If we were to take out all the negative stuff we put in our heads every day and replace it with good, positive information, we would likely be shocked at what we could create and how different our world would be. Once again, we attract whatever is on the same frequency we are on. Our programming tells us that it is normal to complain about our lives because someone always has it better than we do. What our programming does not tell us is what to do about it. Changing our lives is simply a choice.

The Power of the Spoken Word

Limiting beliefs show up in all areas of our lives, including our speech. If you listen to people speak and pay attention to the words they use, you'll probably notice that the majority of people have a very limiting vocabulary. For example, next time you are in a conversation with one of your friends, listen to how many times you hear the word "need" or "can't." I think you will be quite surprised at what you find.

These two words are used so often that hardly anyone gives them a second thought. The reality is that they may be playing a huge part in why you are not reaching your true potential. There is incredible power in the spoken word, and you can literally speak your consciousness into existence. It is not uncommon to hear someone say, "I *can't* afford that . . ." or "I *need* to work this weekend . . ." These are disempowering statements that bring negative results and poverty into your life. There is enormous power in your vocabulary, and when you begin to use empowering words in your speech, you will quickly see the difference in your reality.

The following is a list of disempowering words as well as a list of corresponding empowering words that you may choose to implement into your daily vocabulary. Changing your vocabulary is the first step to getting rid of old limiting beliefs so that you can create a life that was designed for you and by you.

Disempowering Words	Empowering Words
"Can't"	"Can," or "How can I"
"Need"	"Deserve"
"Want"	"Will" or "Have"
"Try"	"Do"
"Hope"	"Will"
"Don't have"	"Will have"
"Wish"	"Expect"

These are some of the most common disempowering words that people use and the empowering words that can replace them. If you are truly committed to maximizing the potential in yourself and in life, your journey must begin here. The vocabulary you use is simply a form of energy, and by law, energy always returns to its source of origination.

One of the universal laws, the law of cause and effect, states that everything is energy. All things are energy in different states of vibration, and whatever energy you put out will come back to you, in most cases tenfold. If you put out negative energy, you can expect negative energy to come back to you. That energy may be in any number of forms, physical or emotional.

On the contrary, should you put out positive energy, you will receive positive energy in return, also tenfold. The really great thing about energy is that it is not restricted by physical boundaries. If all things are energy and all matter vibrates at a particular frequency, thought energy must be the highest frequency energy of all.

The Law of Vibration

The way energy works is simple and it has a powerful effect on your everyday life. All matter is energy in a constant state of vibration. You are a mass of energy and you vibrate at a given frequency. Your frequency can change with your thoughts, feelings, and actions. Your results in life are directly related to your frequency because you, as a mass of energy, will attract whatever energy is on the same frequency you are on.

What that means is that you will not attract that which you want, but that which you are. In other words, if you're getting crappy results in life, it's because you're putting out crappy energy. You have probably heard the old saying, "I'll believe it when I see it." Actually, that's not the way the universe works. Rather, "You'll see it when you believe it."

You may think this all sounds kind of hokey, so let me give you an example. The energy you're putting out could be in the form of thoughts, feelings, actions, intentions, or behavior. For example, have you ever been driving in traffic and had someone either cut you off or sit through a green arrow in front of you because they were not paying attention? I'm sure most of us have experienced this.

When this happens, how do you react? Do you yell and cuss and send hand signals or do you remain calm and realize that yelling at the person will not change a thing? Think about that for a second and answer honestly. Speaking for myself, I know that it's not easy to maintain composure in situations like these. If you are someone who reacts with yelling and hand signals, you are in a negative or low vibration and putting out a negative energy, which will come back to you in the form of a negative result one way or another.

If you are a person who remains calm and accepts the fact that some people are just not very courteous or do not pay attention, you will remain in a higher vibration, thus emitting positive energy. When your vibration remains at a high frequency, you send out positive energy and thus you will get back positive energy in the form of some positive result. Someone once said, "If you'll set yourself on fire with excitement, people will come from all over to watch you burn." Most of them will pay good money for it, too.

With all that said, take a look at yourself and think for a moment about where you are in your life in relationship to where you would like to be. Are you there? Are you close? If not, evaluate your daily life as well as the energy you are putting out and see if you don't notice a correlation between your energy and your results. Hint: this can be a humbling process, so you must be authentic and you must be able to own what you see. Don't make excuses.

Take a look at Anthony Robbins. If you haven't ever seen him either on TV or live, order one of his videos or DVD's and watch this guy's energy. It is amazing. He has passion oozing out of him in the form of speech and his overall energy. The guy is on fire all the time. The reason I bring this up is that Tony knows the power of positive vibration and that is exactly what has gotten him to the level of success he enjoys.

If you are one of those people like I was several years ago when I first heard about this idea of personal development, you're probably thinking, "Who needs that stuff? I'm fine the way I am; it's the rest of the world that's screwed up." I thought I was too macho to be involved with something that sounded so feminine. The truth was, I was too scared to take a look at the real me. I knew I wouldn't like what I saw.

The funny part was, when I finally gave it a chance and admitted that things were not working very well the way I was doing them and I started to apply these ideas in my life, I saw huge changes in my results. I began a home-based business that made almost four hundred thousand dollars the first year. My advice to you is, do not let your pride stand in the way of creating the life of your dreams. The definition of insanity is doing the same thing over and over and expecting a different result.

The whole world is at your disposal, and you can create anything you want for yourself and your life. All you have to do is learn to change the way you think. The way I used to look at life was that there was a pie and I was allowed to have a piece. However, I could only have a tiny sliver because I had to allow everyone else to have his or her piece of the pie, too. What I've learned is, if I want a bigger piece of the pie, I can just create a bigger pie. Wanting a bigger piece does not mean someone else has to get a smaller piece. It is not greedy to desire more. It only becomes greed when you take from someone else in order to have more.

Think of it like this: you can live your life on a creative plane or on a competitive plane; it is your choice. I choose to live on a creative plane. If you live on the competitive plane, you are living your life with lack, limitation, and fear. Those three traits lead to a life of poverty and dismay. On the other hand, living on the creative plane leaves the door open for prosperity and wealth. Creativity allows you to have as much pie as you want without taking anything away from others. Remember, the surest way to get what you want in life is to help others get what they want.

THE LAW OF OPPOSITES

The last law I would like to cover in this section is the law of opposites, sometimes called the law of polarity. The law of opposites could very well be the missing piece in many people's success puzzle. This law states that you cannot have an up without a down, an in without an out, a light without a dark, or a negative without an equal or greater positive. Because of the way we become conditioned to challenges and set-backs in life, many people choose to focus on the negatives in life, not realizing that for every negative there is also an equal or greater positive. You've heard the old saying, "When one door closes, another door opens."

This is the law of opposites. The problem is, when that door closes, and it will close many times during your life, some people tend to focus on that closed door. They stress and worry and think, "Oh no . . . what am I going to do now?"

This type of reactive behavior is the norm. What they don't realize is that while they are doing all of that, the open door, or should I say the opportunity, is right behind them, for they never turn around to look for it.

You must realize that there is always a positive that comes along with a negative. It has to be that way. It's a universal law. In order for us to be able to see the opportunities and open doors, we must first understand that they are always there.

Second, we must know how to look for and spot them. They will rarely be in plain sight surrounded by flashing lighted signs that say, "Open Door to Opportunity—This Way."

Obviously this is a ridiculous example, but the principle remains the same. When you run into challenges in your life, why not look for the opportunity that you now know is there by law rather than spending valuable time focusing on the challenge itself?

Expect Success

To have success in any area of your life takes more than a few universal laws and some personal development. All the personal development in the world will not help you if you don't believe in yourself. You have to expect the success you seek.

Several years ago when I first began working for myself, I struggled to have even a small amount of success. One day my mentor, the person who introduced me to personal development, called and asked me if I knew why I wasn't having success. I replied by saying that I did not know, so he informed me that the reason I was not having success was that I didn't expect it. My first reaction was to argue and defend myself, but instead of arguing I thought about what he said, only to find that he was right. I did not expect to have success.

I had been marketing a product I didn't expect people to buy. My belief in myself was not strong enough for me to see people actually getting involved with what I had to offer. This is a perfect example of the subconscious mind giving me exactly what I asked for. I had given my energy to the fact that people would not purchase this product based on my old conditioning. I told myself, "It's too expensive; people are not going to spend this much; blah, blah, blah." Remember, what you give energy to is what the subconscious sees as reality. The subconscious only knows what you tell it. My subconscious heard me telling it that I expected to fail. So my subconscious mind said, "He's asking to fail, he expects to fail, so that's what I'll give him."

At that moment, I changed my attitude and my mindset about my business. What I had been missing all along was confidence. Once I realized I could have the same confidence as a successful leader, I began to see the results of a successful leader. The next month my business made thirty-five thousand dollars profit within thirty days. Expecting success made all the difference in the world.

CONFIDENCE

The reason I was able to see such a dramatic change in my result was simply that I was able to find confidence in what I was doing. How does a person get the confidence to have success? One of the reasons people may not have confidence may simply come from a lack of education or information regarding a particular subject. If we do not have enough information about a particular topic, most likely we will not have the confidence to get up and speak or even make decisions about that topic.

Think of an area of your life in which you have plenty of confidence. It may be cooking, cars, computers, painting, dancing, or any number of other possibilities. Everyone has something they are confident about. I had a woman tell me one time that she had confidence in being a good parent. That's great! It does not matter what area it is you have confidence in, only that you think of something that you are confident about.

Now think about how you would feel if someone were to come up and ask you for information about the particular subject you are confident about. Could you have a conversation about the subject? Would you be able to answer their questions or at least help them to know where to get their questions answered? My bet is that you would not have any trouble doing so.

What I would like you to think of now is how you feel on the inside when you are speaking about your subject. Do you feel powerful, strong? Is your posture more upright? Does your voice have more volume, power, and conviction than normal? Is there passion and energy when you speak? If you are like me when I speak about something I am confident about, I definitely have conviction in my voice and people do not have to wonder if I know what I'm talking about.

There are two areas in my life that far exceed all other areas for the amount of passion and confidence I have. One is flying airplanes and the other is skydiving. However, just to let you know, I never do them both at the same time. As a pilot, I have about six thousand hours of flight time and I have worked as a professional pilot for several years. As a skydiver, I have almost seven thousand jumps. The reason I am using these examples is that I know how I feel inside when I speak about either one. If you should ever hear me speak about either of these topics, you'd hear the passion in my voice. I'm sure you can relate something in your life to the feelings I'm talking about. Chances are, it is probably one of those things that you could talk about for hours.

For now, I will use flying to illustrate my point about confidence. When I was hired for my first job as a passenger charter pilot, I had to take a check-ride with an examiner from the Federal Aviation Administration. It's similar to taking your driver's test, only the examiners are not nearly as friendly. The day I was scheduled to take my check-ride I was very nervous, as this was my first real job.

I finished the three-hour oral exam just fine and then we were set to head out to the airplane for the flight portion. When a pilot takes a check-ride for a charter pilot job, he or she flies most of the one- to three-hour flight portion under what is called a hood. This means flying without being able to see out the window, flying strictly by reference to the flight instruments. As I began this portion of my check-ride, I was again feeling nervous. We were about thirty minutes into the flight and I found myself making mistakes I would normally not make. Somewhere around the third or fourth mistake, the examiner said, "Why don't we go on back to the airport and talk about this?" I knew right then the ride was over and I had failed.

When we got back to the airport, we went into the conference room and the examiner said, "You know what your problem is? You've got no confidence. You're a great pilot and you know what you're doing; you just don't have the confidence to do it." He went on to say, "I'd suggest you put a little chip on your shoulder and fly like you know how, or you're going to kill yourself and possibly someone else."

To this day, that has been some of the most valuable advice I have ever received. It has not only made me a better pilot, it has also made me a better person all around, for it applies to virtually all areas of my life.

The examiner told me he would be leaving to grab some lunch and when he came back, we were going to go out and do the flight portion again and he did not want to see the same person flying. While he was gone, I thought about the advice he had given me. The more I thought about his words, the more I realized I really was a good pilot and I didn't have to second-guess myself.

After lunch, we went back to the airplane and took off for the flight portion. The entire flight took about two hours and went perfectly. I flew better than I had ever flown before. It felt so good to know that I had the power and skill within me all along. That confidence has since carried over into my business and my personal life and has been a huge factor in my successes.

Now let's go back to you and your life. You have thought of something you are confident about in some area of your life. What I would like you to do now is think of an area in your life that you would like to have the same level of confidence in. For example, maybe you would like to be better in sales or perhaps you want to be more confident in investing. Whatever you choose, make sure it is something at the opposite end of the spectrum from what you picked for having confidence.

First, it is not necessary for you to know all the answers to have the confidence you seek. Maybe you can read some books or talk to someone you know who can help you get a better understanding of the topic or area you would like more confidence in. The important thing to remember is that confidence comes from you and no one else. Here is how you can trick yourself into that confidence: take a piece of paper and draw a line down the middle, longways, so you have two columns. At the top of the left column, write "Successful Person." At the top of the right column, write "Me." Now, in the left column, begin to list all the qualities you believe a successful person has. If you would like to use yourself and the area you have confidence in, do so.

Successful Person	*Me*
1. _____	1. _____
2. _____	2. _____
3. _____	3. _____
4. _____	4. _____
5. _____	5. _____
6. _____	6. _____
7. _____	7. _____
8. _____	8. _____
9. _____	9. _____
10. _____	10. _____

As you list those qualities, challenge yourself to come up with every possible trait a successful person would have. Begin to build the perfect successful person in your mind. How would this person walk? How would this person talk?

What would this person wear? How would this person carry him or herself in a group setting?

Once you have a list of five to ten traits that you believe describe the perfect successful person, move to the other side of the paper and see how many of those qualities from the left side of the page also fit on the right. Do you have any of those qualities? If you do, that's awesome. If you do not, that's okay, too. I am going to show you how to get all of the qualities listed on the left side of the paper over to the right.

AFFIRMATIONS

There are two ways to effect a change on the subconscious mind. One is through emotional impact and the other is through repetition. These visualization and affirmation exercises are the way to use repetition.

Along with visualization, you can also use positive affirmations to help you reach your goals. If you have never used affirmations before, they are very simple and they work. An affirmation is simply a thought or suggestion you give your subconscious mind for the purpose of reprogramming it. It is important to remember that your subconscious mind does not know the difference between the truth and a lie—it has no ability to reject anything. The subconscious accepts everything it receives as reality. Knowing this, a person can actually trick the subconscious mind into achieving literally anything the person would like.

The reason this is so important is that if you keep giving your subconscious mind negative input, you will continue to get negative results. Using positive affirmations on a regular basis is a way to make the subconscious believe that what you're telling it is already reality. Once the subconscious has the thought or idea, it is simply a matter of time before that thought or idea manifests into physical form. Whatever you give to your subconscious mind will become reality, so be careful what you let in.

Some great affirmations I used when I was marketing were simple statements about the reality I held in my mind:

- I am a multiple-six-figure income earner and I help people all over the country improve the quality of their lives.
- I am the top income earner in my company.
- I drive an E55 and I live in a beautiful home overlooking the mountains.
- I am a best-selling author and speaker and my work helps people all over the world.

As a little side note, I have achieved all of these goals with the exception of "best-selling author." However, I expect that to happen shortly.

Visualization

As children, most of us went through a phase where we sat and daydreamed glorious fantasies. As children, we were born with this natural ability to visualize. We dreamed of being astronauts or princesses, cowboys or actresses. We took marvelous trips in our minds to exotic places where everything we sought was at our disposal. These childhood daydreams were common up to the point when our parents or teachers informed us, "Daydreaming is for kids" and we were told we had to grow up and be more responsible.

Our parents called what we were doing daydreaming, but it was indeed visualization, and this basic form of visualizing was the start of creating any reality we desired. Though it came to a screeching halt when we were told to quit doing it, we can relearn how to visualize.

I touched on this in the first section, but I'd like to take you through a full exercise. This requires you to be in a comfortable place such as a recliner or an office chair with no outside distractions such as people talking, dogs barking, or kids playing. It is also important that you are relaxed and not thinking about anything that causes you stress. I want you to relax, close your eyes, and picture yourself in the future. How far in the future is up to you. It may be a year or ten years; what is important is how you see yourself at that point in the future. I want you to picture yourself as the perfect leader in the particular area you have indicated you would like to have more confidence in.

In a sense, what we are about to do is to build you into the perfect leader, just the way we would order a custom luxury automobile built just for you according to your specifications. Here, everything is up to you. You get to design *you* the way you want to be. In your mind, I want you to see yourself as the person who has all the qualities you have listed on the left side of your paper.

The trick is to visualize yourself as already having all these qualities. Notice how you walk, talk, the clothes you wear, and the car you drive. Notice your posture both physically and emotionally. See how you carry yourself in all situations. Keep going over this image in your mind until you can call it up at will and see yourself as this leader. Make sure you relate this person to your business and the results you want in your business. You may have to spend some time in the beginning to get it in your mind so you can actually see it and remember it. Do this visualization process as many times as necessary until you can call this image up at will. The more you perform these steps, the longer this image will stay with you and the more it will become a part of you. Eventually, you will become this person.

What you are doing is reprogramming your subconscious mind with a new self-image. Your subconscious mind does not know the difference between the truth and a lie. Your subconscious mind accepts everything you give it as fact. Anything you give energy to—good or bad, positive or negative—will go into your subconscious mind as fact. Your subconscious will then take the necessary steps to manifest those details into physical form.

Have you ever heard someone use the phrase "worry yourself sick" or "worry yourself to death"? Where do you think they come from? They refer to what is known as psychosomatic illnesses, pains in the body caused by the mind. The subconscious mind has the power to create anything. You and your conscious mind are the gatekeepers to your subconscious. Make sure you closely monitor what is going into your subconscious mind. It's like a fertile garden—whatever you plant will grow. With that in mind, wouldn't it make sense to plant only that which will give you the life of your dreams?

Now that you have this image in your mind of yourself as the perfect leader, visit the image as often as possible. I recommend spending a few minutes three or four times per day visualizing the image of you as this leader. Make sure you start your day and end your day with this visualization exercise.

After you've had a chance to do the exercise several times, go back to the right- hand column and begin to transfer the qualities from the left side of the paper to the right side as you begin to see each of the qualities come to life in you. Before long, you will have built yourself into the perfect leader with only the power of your subconscious mind.

GOAL SETTING

Now that you have seen yourself in the future, let's take these visions and put them into a written format that we will refer to as your goals. Goal setting is a powerful technique that can be used to help you achieve all the things you want in life. Most people simply wish they had a better life or a different result, but unfortunately, wishes rarely come true. The key to making goal setting work is to add emotion to your goals.

When you visualize or do affirmations, you must add powerful emotion to the mix. This will tell the subconscious mind that what you are visualizing or verbalizing is one hundred percent real. The subconscious mind does not know the difference between a truth and a lie, so whatever you give your energy to is what will manifest in your life.

There are different methods to figuring out what your goals are. One of the most common methods is the SMART method. This acronym will help you make sure your goals are set with the best chance of achieving them. This is the format for a SMART goal:

S – Specific—make sure you know exactly what you want to achieve.

M– Measurable—your goal should be something that will allow you to track progress.

A– Attainable—your goal should be something you can achieve. Don't set a goal to achieve something in a year that you know will take ten years.

R – Realistic—be sure the goal is something that can be accomplished in your mind. Do not worry what other people say. It only matters that it is real in your mind.

T – Time—be sure to put a time on your goal. Remember, work expands for the time allotted. By setting sharp, clearly defined goals, you can measure and take pride in the achievement of these goals. You can see forward progress in what might previously have seemed a long, pointless grind.

By setting goals and measuring their achievement, you are able to see what you have done and what you are capable of. The process of achieving goals and seeing their achievement gives you the confidence and self-belief you need to know you will be able to achieve higher and more difficult goals.

Once you have set your lifetime goals, set a twenty-five-year plan of smaller goals that should be achieved if you are to reach your lifetime plan. Then set a five-year plan, a one-year plan, a six-month plan, and a one-month plan of progressively smaller goals that should be reached to achieve your lifetime goals.

Finally, set a daily to-do list of things you should do today to achieve your lifetime goals. At this stage, many goals may simply be to read books and gather information on the achievement of your goals so that you can improve the quality and realism of your goal setting. Last, review your plans and make sure they fit the way you want to live your life.

Once you have decided your first goal plans, keep the process going by reviewing and updating your to-do list on a daily basis. Some people recommend doing this as the last thing done before bed, others as the first thing done each morning. It's up to you. Periodically review your other plans and modify them to reflect your changing priorities.

When you achieve a goal, take time to enjoy the satisfaction of having achieved it. Absorb the implications of the goal achievement and observe the progress you have made towards other goals.

If the goal is a significant one or one you have worked toward for some time, take the opportunity to reward yourself appropriately after you have achieved it.

To properly set a goal, you must be very specific about what your goal is. It's not enough to write, "I want a new car." You must know exactly what car you want, what color, what year, what interior, what engine, and so on. For example:

> *By October 1, 2006, I will own a new 2007, black BMW M5 with tan leather interior, eight-speaker Bose sound system, and GPS navigation system. I will achieve this goal by helping fifty people improve the quality of their lives in the next three months, thereby earning me an income of $125,000.*

You can also write your goals in present tense as if they have already manifested. For example:

> *October 1, 2006: I am so happy and grateful now that I have helped fifty people improve the quality of their lives through my business. I have generated an income of $125,000 in return and am now enjoying my new 2007, black BMW M5 with tan leather interior, eight-speaker Bose sound system, and GPS navigation system.*

That is what a goal should look like. After writing your goals, keep a copy in your pocket at all times as well as a copy in a place where you will see it every day, such as above your desk, on the refrigerator, or on the bathroom mirror. It is vitally important that you read these goals every day without fail. Make sure when you read them that you do so out loud with plenty of powerful emotion.

I've included a goal contract form in the appendix, which is a great way to keep track of your goals. A goal contract looks just like a real, binding contract. The only difference is that the goal contract is a contract with yourself. I recommend treating this contract just the way you would any binding contract that you sign.

I keep my goal contracts in two different three-ring binders. One binder is called "Current Goals" and the other binder is "Achieved Goals." When I write a new goal, it goes into the "Current Goals" book. It remains there until I have achieved the goal. At that time, I move the goal contract to the "Achieved Goals" book. If I should ever have "one of those days" when I don't feel like I'm reaching my goals, I just open up the "Achieved Goals" book and flip through all the goals I have already achieved. This is both inspiring and motivating.

Don't hesitate to start your "Achieved Goals" book by filling it with goals that you have already achieved up to this point in your life. It's motivating, and it will recharge you when you're having "one of those days," so use it. It really works!

Once you have your goal in written form, I recommend that you go find your goal in physical form if possible, in this case a new M5. Touch it, feel it, smell it. Let all your senses absorb the object of your goal. Get inside and see how it feels around you. How does it smell? What does it sound like when you start it up? How does it respond when you drive it? How does the stereo system sound?

If your goal is a new home, go find the home you want, or one very close to it, and walk through it. Take pictures of your new home. Get to know every room in your home. Mentally put your furniture, or the furniture you will have, in each of the rooms just the way it will be when it's yours. Take in all the sites, smells, and feelings that the home brings to your senses. Visit your home often, and each time you walk through it, see yourself doing all the things you would be doing if you were living there right now. These are all things that will help you manifest your goals into reality.

The key to making these visualization sessions work is to take possession of the goal that you desire in your mind. It's a way to take mental ownership of the object or goal. This is all part of the process of reprogramming your subconscious mind.

CHAPTER 2 SUMMARY

$\mathcal{S}$uccess starts in the subconscious mind before anything is ever manifested into reality. You can be, do, and have anything you want for yourself and your life simply by learning how to manifest it through the power of your subconscious mind. The great thing about your subconscious mind is that it doesn't know the difference between the truth and a lie. The subconscious mind only knows what you tell it. If you tell your subconscious mind that you are the top income earner in your company often enough, with powerful emotion and conviction, your subconscious mind will see that as reality and will create the conditions necessary for that to manifest into physical form. There are several things to consider as you begin the process of reprogramming your subconscious mind:

FEAR is an acronym for False Expectations Appearing Real. Most people have FEAR due to a lack of information about a particular subject. Once you learn how to move past your FEAR, you will be able to achieve levels of success that you previously did not believe were possible.

Limiting beliefs are unwanted gifts given to us by the people closest to us. You can replace limiting beliefs with a new belief system through visualization and positive affirmations.

Everything is energy. You will attract that which is on the same frequency you are on. Your results will be directly related to the vibration you are in. If you are getting unwanted results, take a look at the energy you are putting out into the universe.

Thoughts have power. Your thoughts are one of the most powerful forms of energy in existence. What you spend your time thinking about will manifest in your life. If you worry about things not working out, things will tend not to work out. If you see all challenges as opportunities, you will generally get positive results out of most challenges.

Your words have power, and you can speak your reality into existence. The words you use every day shape the world you are in. Make your vocabulary full of power and prosperity and get rid of words like "can't," "need," "want," "if," "try," "hope," and "wish."

There cannot be a negative without an equal or greater positive. This is the law of opposites, which states that you cannot have a light without a dark, a negative without an equal or greater positive. The key is that you have to know the positives are there. Once you know they are there, you will know to always look for them.

Expect success. Remember, you get what you focus on, so by focusing only on success, you will be removing all other options from the equation. *See only success!*

You can borrow confidence from yourself. Think of an area of your life that you have confidence in, something you are really good at. Take a look at yourself and the energy you have when you speak about that subject. Notice the way you posture yourself when you speak to someone. You can borrow that same confidence and put it to use in other areas of your life as well.

Goals should be specific, measurable, attainable, realistic, and time-based. Become a disciplined goal setter and a goal getter!

Chapter 3

Getting Down to Business

THE COMPANY

Before you become an associate or affiliate with any network marketing company, there are a few things to consider. First of all, you will want to research the company thoroughly to ensure that it is reputable and in good standing with all local, state, and government agencies.

Unfortunately, some companies are less than ethical. They may look attractive up-front, but be careful. You could be getting into a whole lot more than you bargained for. While you are doing your research on the company, make sure you take time to check out its product or service. Make sure it's something you can feel good about marketing. After all, it's going to be your name attached to it when you talk to your clients and associates. If you do not feel good about your product or service, don't expect to have any amount of success. Even if you do, it will be at the expense of your conscious.

Another source of information you can access while you are researching the company and the products and/or services is other associates. You will most likely attend a couple of business opportunity presentations, either live or conference call, so while you are there make sure you speak with as many people as you can. Keep in mind that some of the people you speak with will be veterans and some will be new, so you will get a wide variety of feedback.

Most importantly, don't hesitate to ask questions about how other associates are doing and how they feel about the company. It's up to you after that to put all the information together to build an accurate picture of the opportunity as a whole. As far as the company is concerned, you may want to consider whether it is a private company or a publicly-traded company. There are considerations to both, so make sure you understand the difference and what it means to the associates. While I cannot advise you one way or the other, I have been with both types of companies and the differences between the two can be substantial. It's up to you to determine which is best for you.

Last, I recommend taking a good look at the compensation plan the company has in place. This is one of the most important things to consider when researching a company. Does the compensation plan fit you? Some compensation plans are designed to make large profits with fewer sales, and some will generate smaller profits with many sales. Some plans will allow you to be paid directly by the customer, while others have the customer paying the company and then the company cutting you a check. It all boils down to your personal preference.

YOUR ADVISOR

Now that you have done your research and have decided which company you would like to be a part of, your next step is to meet your advisor. I'm going to refer to this person as an advisor for simplicity, but depending on the company you are with, this person might be called the director, scholar, sponsor, or possibly something else. They are all names for the same thing—your up line. What you may not know is that with most companies, you have the ability to choose your advisor. Chances are, they are not going to tell you that because it does cause some commotion, but you can do it.

The reason I bring this up is that if you want to make it to the top income earner position, you are going to want to enroll with someone who is a leader, and I don't just mean financially. You need someone who can lead and who will be there after you've signed and paid.

If you were going to become a surgeon and were interviewing people to train you, you wouldn't just blindly accept that the first person you spoke with was the best person for the job, would you? Wouldn't you want to know that this person truly knew what he or she was doing and that they could train you well?

This is no different. Unfortunately, some associates get started with an advisor who has been in the business ten minutes longer than they have, yet they trust that advisor to have all the answers and usually follow that person's direction, right or wrong, without question.

I'm not suggesting that if a person gets started with an advisor who is new that they will not have success, but wouldn't you want to give yourself the best possible chance of success?

Take some time and find out who the leaders are. Again, when I say "leaders," I don't just mean who makes the most money. I mean who has the most associates making six figures. That's how you identify the leaders. Barring any personality conflicts, the person who has the most associates making six-figure incomes is likely the person I would want to work with.

The Plan

Now that you've set some goals, you'll want to meet with your advisor to review your goals and start developing a plan of how you're going to work your business. A thorough planning session with your advisor is well warranted at this time. Time spent here in the beginning will save you an exponential amount of time later. Nonetheless, sometimes this is easier said than done. The challenge with many advisors is that they get so slammed with their own business that they have a challenge finding time to take care of their associates. If you run into this situation, remember this—the squeaky wheel gets the grease. If you call your advisor and don't get a call back, keep calling. Too many times, a new associate will call once and when they don't get a call back, they just quit calling.

I promise that if you do that, you will not be accepting any awards the first month. You have to let your advisor know you are serious and that you expect to be the best with their help. If you approach it this way, you'll have better results getting them to call you back. Speaking from experience, I know that advisors get countless calls from associates for every reason under the sun, and sometimes advisors have to prioritize their call-backs according to who they believe is the most serious about their business.

You and your advisor should also discuss what kind of marketing and advertising you're going to start off with according to the budget you have to work with. Some network marketing companies have lead programs in place so their associates do not have to worry about lead generation. These lead programs are generally set up where you buy your leads in bulk. Most lead programs allow you to purchase leads in quantities like 25, 50, 100, 250, 500, 1,000, and so on. If your company has such a program in place, check with your advisor to see how the system works and if there are any requirements or minimums for you to purchase.

LEAD BROKERS

If your company does not have a lead program in place but you would still like to purchase your leads, there are some things you should be familiar with before making your first purchase. First, this is an avenue to take if you want leads to contact right now. Generally, lead companies can get you your leads within one to twenty-four hours. If you are going to use lead brokers (i.e., buy your leads), understand that these people are in the business to make money. The leads you get from a lead broker or lead company will not be the same quality as the leads coming from an ad that you personally place, regardless of what the salesperson tells you.

They will, however, teach you to be resilient and proficient. Most lead companies have their leads broken down into price categories by how old the lead is and how it was generated. In most cases, you will not be able to tell the difference from one category to the next.

Before we talk about what you will experience when you buy leads, let me share with you how lead companies generate their leads. If you talk to a representative from a lead company, you will be told their leads are "pre-qualified" and they go through a "multi-step qualification process" that allows them to "almost" guarantee their leads. They will tell you that if you get any wrong or disconnected numbers, they will replace them two-for-one in return. The lead company representative will most likely tell you that these leads have never been sold to anyone else, or at least not to anyone in "your" company. Basically, you will get a fifteen-minute dissertation on why their leads are the best.

Here is what actually happens: these lead companies get their leads from one of two places. Either they generate their leads through their own in-house ads, which is rare, or they buy them from another company that generates them and then they mark up the price and sell them to you. If the lead company generates their leads in-house, the leads come from tons of very general "biz op" ads or "work from home" ads in various publications from newspapers to magazines to Internet sites. As people respond to these ads the company gathers the prospects' contact information and then sells that information to you in the form of a lead. The problem comes when that lead sits for 30, 90, or even 180 days. In addition, that lead may have been sold 25 or even 50 times before you buy it.

This does not mean there are not some good and reputable lead companies out there. At the same time, I must tell you that in my almost ten years in the industry, I have purchased thousands and thousands of leads and I have yet to find a company that can deliver what they promise.

There is a positive side to this: buying leads is a <u>great</u> way to supplement any of your other lead generation sources. The other great thing about buying leads is that they are great for training yourself or your associates to become better at prospecting. If you can become proficient at prospecting purchased bulk leads, you will be great when you are talking to a prospect who has actually responded to an ad you have placed.

What you will experience when you call leads from a lead broker is mostly frustration. Keep in mind, however, that within all that frustration may be a gold mine just waiting for you to call. You must remember that while you are prospecting these leads, or you may very well toss your stack of leads right into the trash after the first hour. As I said, I have purchased thousands of leads through these types of companies and generally I get a high percentage (forty to sixty percent) of either disconnected or wrong numbers.

When I call and get a wrong number, I almost always hear something like, "I told you people to stop calling here. For the last time, John doesn't live here and I didn't respond to any ad!" Sometime colorful adjectives are often thrown in as well, but I'll leave those out for this example. If you have had the opportunity to call any brokered leads, this example probably sounds very familiar.

Responses like the one I've just described are a very good indication that your "pre-qualified" leads have been sold to several other people besides yourself. Now, with all that said, understand that this is just the way it is with purchased leads. If you are going to use them, this is how it will be. Just keep pushing through your list until you find that gold mine I mentioned.

Purchased leads, in my opinion, should never be your only source of leads. I recommend using at least three sources of lead generation at any given time. The goal is never to have fewer than 100 to 150 leads on your desk. If you are not able to use that many leads, I recommend sharing some with your associates.

VOICEMAIL

After you have had a chance to sit down with your advisor, either in person or over the phone, and have discussed getting started, it is time to add some housekeeping items. In this business, regardless of the company you choose to work with, there isn't much overhead. It is truly one of the most attractive benefits of this type of business that you can work right out of your home with little or no overhead. What little overhead there may be can be the difference between making a six-figure income and making next to nothing.

The first thing I recommend is setting up an 800 voicemail. Some companies will have this in place as part of their "back office" or they may have a particular voicemail company they want their associates to use, so check with your advisor before signing up for a service.

There are a couple of primary reasons to use an 800 voicemail service. First of all, an 800 number gives you instant credibility. 800 numbers are professional, and if you are advertising outside your local area, your prospects will appreciate your having it. Some people will not respond to an ad if it requires a long distance call.

Another reason to use an 800 voicemail is so your phone doesn't ring off the wall at home. If you are running even moderate amounts of advertising, your phone will be ringing more than you will be able to keep up with. You don't want to lose potential sales because your prospects can't get through, not to mention that it will drive you crazy. With an 800 number, the person calling will never get a busy signal regardless of how many people are responding to the ad at the same time.

800 voicemail services also allow you to use an outgoing message on the voicemail, which will help you weed out tire-kickers and people who are not serious and do nothing but waste your time. With many 800 voicemail companies, you can access your messages on-line to see how many calls you've had and can even listen to your messages on-line, which doesn't count against your minutes. There are many different voicemail companies out there, some with much more to offer than others. Your advisor will have the information on the currently recommended company.

If your company does not endorse or recommend a particular voicemail company, make sure you do your homework and research several companies before signing up or enrolling. Some companies are better than others, and some have many more usable features and benefits. Be sure to look for and ask about any long-term commitments, set-up fees, hidden fees, cancellation fees, billing options, access options, roll-over minutes, referral programs (a fee paid to you for your associates), affiliate programs (a separate income stream for you), and most of all, be sure to read any fine print that may be available before you sign up.

Business Cards

After your voicemail is set up, you'll want to order some business cards. Even if it is your intention to work strictly on the Internet and not do any personal contact marketing, business cards are still great to have. In my opinion, they are a must. I once had a month where I made $35,000 profit using nothing but business cards. So, as you might guess, I feel pretty strongly about them.

Inevitably, you will meet people who ask what you do for a living. After all, this is a common question. Don't miss out on these potentially hot prospects because you only want to market on the Internet. As I said, you should always be utilizing at least three forms of lead generation at any one time. Personal contact marketing, or PCM, is one of the most productive and powerful forms of lead generation you can use. (PCM will be thoroughly covered in Chapter Four.)

Having a business card to give someone who may ask about your business or what you do for a living is just smart business. Again, it's instant credibility in the eyes of a prospect. If you are utilizing live business presentations, you will definitely want business cards to give to your guests when they show up at your presentations. If you are using a live or recorded conference call system, you can send your guests a thank you card for attending a call and include your business card with the note.

There are other creative ways to market and use business cards that I will cover more when we get to the section on PCM. The bottom line is, there is no valid reason for not having business cards. They are a part of doing business, regardless of what type of business you are in, and they can make you a ton of money as well. Before I wrap up about business cards, I would like to cover some important do's and don'ts regarding business cards.

Do's

1. Always use professionally printed business cards. In other words, don't skimp!
2. When using a company logo, get approval from the company.
3. Use the standard format if your company has one in place.
4. Make your business card attractive without being too busy.
5. Use the heaviest stock you can find. I prefer a minimum of 130-pound paper. This will make a definite impression on your prospects, and though it is more expensive, it's well worth it.
6. Order larger quantities to keep the cost down.

continued

7. Always have business cards with you or close to you, regardless of where you are.

8. Always have your office, fax, email, website information, and 800 number on your card.

Don'ts

1. Never use perforated paper in your printer to make your own business cards.

2. Don't use clip-art for your business card.

3. Never use a company logo without approval.

4. Don't print your address or cell phone on your business card.

5. Don't use a glossy coating on your business card. This prohibits you from writing on the card, should you have to.

6. Avoid using larger than stock or double fold cards that are too big to be kept with typical card libraries.

7. Never give out a card if you have previously written something on it. Get a new, clean card.

8. Never leave home without your business cards.

Training and Resources

Most companies have training programs in place for their associates. Some are live, some are on conference calls, and some are online or downloadable. Regardless of what type of training program your company has in place, use it! Within literally any company, you can generally go into a roster of associates and tell who the top income earners are by looking at who attends the most training events. There is a reason companies have these training events—they work.

My First Training

The first training I ever attended was incredibly powerful for me. Not only was I totally captivated by the energy as well as the people, I also got to see all the leaders get up on stage and accept awards for production and perseverance as well as several other awards.

I will never forget that day. As I watched the production from start to finish, I literally sat on the edge of my seat, feeling the power and the rush of emotions as the leaders were called by name to come out of the audience and proceed to the stage where they were presented their awards.

I made myself a promise that day: I would be one of those people. I wanted to feel that sense of accomplishment, that feeling of achievement that would come to me when I was presented an award on stage.

It took about three years to make it happen, but I did it. As I stood on the stage at a beautiful, black-tie event, holding the Top Income Earner Award I had just been presented by the co-founder of the company, I fought back tears and struggled to speak. I looked out over the crowd at my sister Lori and my best friend Bruce sitting in the front row, center stage. All that came to mind was an argument I'd had with my sister about money when I was in college several years before. At that time, in 1991, Lori was a registered nurse in Kansas City making about $40,000 a year, and I was an unemployed, broke college student.

As the argument had progressed and become more heated, I'd said, "Well, that's easy for you to say . . . you make $40,000 a year." The words that came back at me from Lori would haunt me for years, but would also change my life and inevitably be the driving force that got me to the stage that night.

Lori said, "Well, you'll never make $40,000 a year because you can't hold a job!"

The sad part was, she was right. I couldn't hold a job. Every time I got a job, I found a reason not to keep it. The most common reason was simply that I could not handle the fact that someone was sitting behind a desk telling me how much I was worth.

For example, when I was just out of high school, I had a job welding aircraft parts. I was required to be certified and all the parts I welded had to be tested. I made $6/hour, and the guy who swept the floor made $14/hour. In addition, the person who sat beside me doing the exact same job made $27/hour. Tell me, why would I want to keep doing that?

I later went on to college to become a pilot and pursue a professional pilot career. I thought I had found my calling. I still love to fly, but I think there were some things somebody forgot to tell me about the state of the job market for pilots at that time. I left college with a master's degree in aviation safety and enough flight time to get my foot in the door somewhere. After a couple of flight instructor positions, I got my first "real" job flying for a passenger charter company in Texas. The funny part was, and I can laugh about it now, I was flying people all over the country for a whopping $15,000/year.

Think about that for a second. If you were a passenger on my airplane and the person next to you leaned over and said, "Psst . . . hey, did you know the pilot only makes $15,000/year?" Be honest, wouldn't you want me to pull over and let you out?

Generally, companies will have a list of different training resources and events for associates to utilize. Beginning with the simple and working up, there is usually a start-up packet that will list training call schedules, recorded and live, product overview calls, or online streaming video training. Whether the medium is telephone or Internet or CD, DVD, or otherwise, there is normally training in place to cover all the basic start-up items a new associate must contend with.

As a new associate, you'll want to learn as much as you can regarding not only the product but also about working the business. Get on all the training calls as well as any online training events you can. Don't miss any live calls if your company has them. These are an invaluable source of information from people who are having success right now. Spend some time talking to the leaders of the company. Make sure you are at all the training events and introduce yourself to these people. Ask them for any tips they can share on getting started quickly.

In addition to training calls and online events or videos, most companies have regional training events. These events can occur as often as once a month or they might be held quarterly or perhaps even semi-annually. Regardless of how often your company holds these training events, I strongly recommend that you never miss one of these power-packed opportunities to get your business absolutely cranking. These are major events and are generally held at a resort, hotel, or conference center. They are usually all-day and sometimes multi-day events. Aside from the training and information you will receive, there are other reasons not to miss out on these major productions.

These events are great for networking and building relationships with the leaders as well as all of the other associates in the company. These are people you will hear on the calls and possibly see on videos and company promotional material, but rarely have the opportunity to see in person. In most cases, they will be a valuable source of information, and it will help you jump-start your business simply to spend a few minutes with them asking straightforward questions. You'll have the opportunity to make some life-long friendships as well. Since I've been in the industry, I can tell you that some of the best friends I've ever known have come from meeting other associates and leaders at training events around the country.

Weekly Training

By now you've had a chance to research your company, talk to some of the leaders and associates, and you've probably even gotten started. We have discussed several things that should be considered as you are beginning this new business endeavor, and now it's time to jump in and get to work.

Most network marketing companies not only host large national and regional trainings, they also hold weekly trainings for their associates. These weekly trainings could be on a wide variety of topics, and there is probably a training call schedule either in your start-up information or located somewhere in the office of your company/associate website. Ask your advisor for the information on these calls.

As a new associate, these live trainings, which are mostly via conference calls, are your best source of quick information and education on getting your business rolling quickly. There may even be a team training call within your area. Some companies have different teams within the company that hold their own training calls and even small events. Your advisor will be able to tell you if there is a team call in your area.

If there is a team call in your area, your next step is to get on that team call immediately. Most team calls are typically held once a week with a leader in that area as the host. I was part of a group that held a team call on Monday evenings. Regardless of when the call is held, the purpose is to communicate and discuss any pertinent information about your business, up-coming events, and so on.

In addition to the general announcements, the team call will most likely allow you to listen in on live prospecting. This is the first step in your prospecting training. Basically, one of the leaders will call his or her leads live during the team call so that everyone can silently listen in and hear how a prospecting call should sound. The person doing the prospecting will go through a call-back script as you follow along with your script so you can get a feel for the proper way to use a script. (I will cover more on scripts in Chapter Six.) Your advisor will have the information on the phone number, day, and time of the team call. If there is not a team call in your area, why not ask about starting one?

In addition to team calls, many companies also hold product overview calls, live presentation calls, wake-up calls, website training calls, and possibly many others. Again, your advisor will have a call schedule for you if you haven't gotten one already. My rule is this: if there is a call and I'm not in the middle of getting somebody started in my business, I'm on the call. As I said earlier, you can always tell who the top income earners are by looking at who attends the most training events and calls.

Before we move on to the next section, let's quickly see where we are in the process of starting our new business. We have had a chance to sit down with our advisor and discuss just about everything related to getting this business up and running with the exception of how we're going to market. So, in the next chapter, we will concentrate on marketing and advertising. These two areas combined are the lifeline of your business, because if you are not actively engaged in one or both of them, you don't have any leads, and if you don't have leads, you don't have a business.

Before you start marketing, let's quickly review your steps to this point:

1. Research the Company You Are Interested In
   - Speak to other associates and leaders
   - Find out about the product or service

2. Write Down Specific Goals in Your Goal Contract
   - Start from the end and work backwards

3. Meet with Your Advisor
    - Review your goal contract
    - Create a plan of action (The key word is "action"!)
    - Create your marketing and advertising budget

4. Take Care of Housekeeping Issues
    - Set up an 800 number
    - Order your business cards

5. Dial into the Company and Team Training Calls
    - Attend all available training events and calls

6. Establish What Type of Advertising and Marketing You Would Like to Do
    - Establish a budget for advertising

7. Start Marketing

Chapter 3 Summary

*G*etting started in network marketing can be a very rewarding experience, provided you have done some research and have selected a good company with a product or service you feel good about. Remember, some companies have given the industry a black eye because of their unethical practices, so you must do your homework.

- Research companies thoroughly before becoming an associate. Check with local state and federal agencies to affirm that there are no challenges with the company you are interested in or its principals.
- Shop for your advisor. Provided it does not cause problems, look for the person you would like to be mentored by before you get started. Once you enroll, it is most likely too late.
- Develop a clear, concise plan. Spend some time with your advisor or sponsor so you can map out exactly what your plan is to get started and become successful.
- Purchasing leads is a great way to supplement your primary lead generation sources, but make sure you do some research on the lead company before you send them any money.

- Utilize an 800 voicemail number. If your company does not have a 800 voicemail as part of your back office, make sure you get one set up on your own. 800 voicemail service is a powerful tool for your business.
- Always have business cards. They are a sign of professionalism and are a powerful tool for networking and personal contact marketing.
- Training events will shorten your learning curve and they are how the top income earners got to be top income earners. Attending all of the local, regional, and national training events is the best way to learn from those who have already done it and to catch their enthusiasm.

CHAPTER 4

Marketing and Advertising

PERSONAL CONTACT MARKETING

There are many different ways to market your business, and you are only limited by your imagination. One of my favorite ways to market my business costs no money at all. I call it personal contact marketing (PCM). Some people refer to it as the three-foot rule, meaning that anyone who gets within three feet of you is a prospect.

When I first got started in network marketing, my bank account and my wallet were tapped. I scraped together everything I could find just to get started. When it came time to begin advertising, I didn't have two pennies to rub together, let alone enough money to place a three-line ad in the local paper. Rather than sit around twiddling my thumbs, I decided to continue with everything that didn't require money, like going to all the business presentations and getting on all the training calls. At the time, I wasn't taking any guests to the presentations, due to the fact that I didn't have any money to generate leads, or at least that's what I thought at the time. What I began to realize was, it's not necessary to have money to generate leads if you are creative.

One of the trainings I attended gave me an idea. The speaker was talking about marketing and all of the different ways to market. He spent the better part of two hours talking about something he called "your warm market." The challenge with "my warm market" was that I didn't have one. No, really, I didn't know anyone. I had just moved to Arizona and for the most part I didn't know anybody. I certainly didn't have any family to approach, which is actually what got me to thinking. I decided that since I didn't have a warm market, I could just talk to the people I ran into each day. At the very least, I would get to know some people, and I wouldn't alienate my friends and very limited family, which consisted of my sister and my niece.

The reason this worked really well for me was simple. I always went to the presentations and I kept myself very involved with the company and all of the events. This kept me excited all the time. I don't mean that cheesy, overbearing kind of excited. I mean I just had great energy when I spoke to people. I found myself simply going through my daily routine and doing the same things I normally would do. What was different was, people began to approach me and ask me what I was doing and how come I had such great energy all the time. This was an opportunity for me to tell them what I did. The way I use PCM is very simple. As I go through my normal daily activities, whether it's going to the gym, shopping, getting my car washed, and so on, I'm constantly keeping my eyes and ears open for people who are not happy with their present situation. I'm sure you have seen some of these people; they just look like they hate their jobs. These people are everywhere. If I see someone who is obviously not happy or is working on a weekend, I'll ask him or her, "Hey, why are you working on the weekend? You should be home with your family." Or, I might say, "Hey, why are you working on the weekend? You should be out enjoying yourself."

No matter what the person's answer is, it almost always has something to do with not having enough money. Why else do people work two and three jobs? This opens the door for me to hand that person a business card. I'll usually say something like this: "If you're tired of doing this and would like to know how you can make a ton of money working from home, here's my card. Let me get your number and I'll touch base with you in the next day or so and I'll get you some information."

At that point I walk away without saying another word. What that does is eliminate the chance of that person starting to badger me with questions. It also leaves that person with a burning curiosity to know what it is that I do. This is a simple example of how PCM works.

KEYS TO PCM

After a short time, I began to see tremendous success with PCM and almost everybody I spoke with wanted to get started in my business. Before long, I had generated $35,000 in a month just using PCM. I began to get recognition on training calls and at presentations for my success. The more success I had, the more people wanted to know how I was doing it. That got me to thinking, "How was I doing it?" As far as I could tell, I was just going through my daily routine and talking to people. Other associates were calling me almost daily, asking if they could come and follow me for a day to watch me do PCM.

The first time someone asked if they could follow me for a day and watch me, I said "Sure." This is how I learned the secret to being successful at PCM. A woman who was one of my best friends as well as a fellow associate asked if she could ride along with me for the day and learn how to do PCM. I told her we would go to the mall because I had done very well there the previous month. When we got to the mall, we did exactly what I had done before and we just wandered through the various shops browsing and having conversations with people. We must have gone through twenty stores and talked with fifty-plus people. When we walked out of the mall, we had exactly zero prospects and zero business.

To say the least, I was embarrassed and felt like a moron. Here I was, this guy who was having so much success with PCM, and when I took someone out to demonstrate how simple it was, nothing happened. What was going on? I realized that the key to PCM was being natural. You can't force it. That's why nothing happened at the mall—I was trying to force it so she could see how easy it was. If you are going to do PCM and be successful at it, you must be real with people.

When I say "real," I mean you must have a genuine desire to help people and you can't sell them. That may not make any sense to you right now, but I will do my best to make it clear in this section. If you are trying to sell someone because you need the money, forget it. They will see dollar signs in your eyes and they will never bite. We are all in the business of sales. In one way or another, everyone is in sales because nothing happens until someone sells something. The irony is that almost everybody hates to be sold, so what do you do?

I will get into sales techniques more in the chapter on retailing your product or service, but for now let me just say that if you are going to be successful in sales, you must be able to sell without your customer feeling like they are being sold. Also, I highly recommend that you read *How to Master the Art of Selling* by Tom Hopkins. I had the privilege of marketing Tom's one-day seminar for a period of time, and during that time I learned more about sales from Tom and his material than I had ever known previously. I strongly encourage you to read Tom's book and attend his "boot camp" if you are serious about your business.

Unfortunately, most of us have probably had a bad experience with the type of salesperson who gives the rest of the profession a bad name. If you have ever been approached by an overbearing, hard-closing sales professional when you were not even interested in owning, you know how uncomfortable it can be after you've said "No" or "I'm just looking" and the person won't stop. The way to avoid this scenario when doing PCM is to begin with a normal conversation that has nothing to do with sales or your business. Keep in mind that the examples I am sharing with you are for PCM in your network marketing business.

Wherever I go, I talk to people. It's just the way I am. I have come to realize over time that most of the conversations generally center on the same topics: "Who are you? Where are you from? What do you do for a living?" This is actually a good thing because after you have had a few hundred of these conversations, you can start to predict people's responses.

If I go to the gym and see someone who has great energy, I will start a very casual conversation just like I would if I weren't prospecting. After the typical introduction and name exchange, I'm going to ask him either where he is from or what he does for a living. This is not invasive, and people recognize it as friendly conversation. If I ask "Where are you from?" I will get one of two answers: either "From here" or "From somewhere else." If he's from here, my next question is "What do you do for a living?" When he tells me what he does for a living, I can approach that according to his answer.

The clues I am looking for when he tells me what he does for a living are things like workweek (hours), stress level, travel or time away from home, family (does he have kids), and so on. For example, if he's a mortgage broker, he's probably working excessive hours in a high stress environment. Mortgage brokers make respectable money, but most of them work seventy to eighty hours per week, so he is probably not seeing his family as much as he would like. If he has kids, he is not getting to see them grow up. These will be the hot buttons I will use to get his interest.

If he tells me he's from somewhere else, my next question will be "What brought you here?" Nine times out of ten, the answer is going to be "Work." Obviously, if he says work, I will say, "What do you do for a living?" Now we are back to the same place we were in the previous example. After we get to the point where he has told me what he does and I've found his hot buttons, I'm going to ask him, "Have you ever thought about working for yourself?" The most common answer I get to this question is, "Well, sure, but I don't know what I would do."

This is an opportunity to give him a business card and say, "Here's my card . . . if you're serious about that, give me a call—I can help you." Now he is going to start in with questions like, "Well, what do you do?" If you want to answer this question, I recommend saying, "I help people make a ton of money, so if you're serious about changing your situation, call me."

At this point you must do two things or he will never call. First, look at your watch, and second, say, "I'd love to share the details with you right now, but I'm late for an appointment." Now walk away, looking at your watch. The reason you do this is that if you don't, you will be stuck there answering questions about your business and what you do. If you answer any questions at all, I promise that he is going to make a pre-conceived judgment about what you do or your opportunity and he will never call. If you don't answer any questions, he is going to be left wondering about it and he will likely call you just out of curiosity if nothing else.

Some important points to remember when you are doing PCM:

- *Act as if* you have the posture and tone of a busy, successful person, even if you are brand new.
- *Demonstrate confidence.*
- Remember that if you answer any questions, the person will likely make a premature judgment. *If you stumble or stutter, you lose.*
- After you have given your business card to a prospect and asked him or her to call you, *walk away!* If you stand toe-to-toe with the prospect after that, he or she will pin you down with questions and you will likely lose that prospect.
- *Do not prospect in what I call "need mode"!*

Where to Use PCM

One of the biggest reasons I like PCM is that it's adaptable to almost any social situation, which means you can do it almost anywhere. There are many different places to use PCM. For instance, when you go to a restaurant, consider the person waiting on your table. Does this person have great energy?

Most servers and bartenders who work in average to above average sit-down type restaurants have great energy. They work mostly for tips, so they have to be good with people. When you are out at dining establishments such as these, keep in mind that the people serving you would very likely be great in your business. Pay attention the next time you are out and see if most of them don't have great energy and attitudes.

If you see someone like this and would like to share your opportunity with them, I recommend starting with a compliment. Compliment the person on their great smile or their great energy. After some brief conversation, ask that person if they have ever considered working for themselves. Regardless of their answer, you can introduce them to the idea of working from home and making a very significant six-figure income. Either hand them a business card or consider leaving a business card with a brief note on the back, along with the tip. If you choose to leave a card with the tip, I suggest leaving a generous tip. The key to this approach is being authentic. You must have a genuine interest in helping people or you will not have success. People will be able to sense if you're only doing it to make a sale.

Another place I like to use PCM is any place I visit on a regular basis for recreation, relaxation, or financial reasons. For instance, I enjoy going hiking and running on the trails close to my home. I tend to see the same people there every day. Inevitably, someone asks me what I do for a living because I am always there when most people are at work. The same is true for the gym, the pool, and the drop zone where I go skydiving.

I think the funniest place for me to use PCM has been the bank. When I was marketing, I deposited checks almost every day. I usually went to the same branch because I knew most of the tellers and they were accustomed to the large deposits so they didn't require security holds on my deposits. One day I walked up to the window and the young gentleman took my deposit and after looking at it said, "What do you do for a living? I see you in here almost every day with these huge deposits. You have to tell me; what do you do?"

I responded by asking him, "Why? Aren't you happy with what you're doing?"

He informed me that he was not only unhappy, he wasn't making any money, either. I handed him a card and told him to call me and I would be happy to get him some information. I expected that I would be hearing from him within the next day or two. When I got home about ten minutes later, there was already a message from him on my voicemail. I invited him to a presentation that evening and he got started the next day.

As you go through your day, look at all the people who work around you. Many of these people are working in jobs they hate. In Arizona, anybody who works outside in the summertime is a great person to talk to, in my opinion. One day not too long after I started having success with PCM, I walked out of my apartment and saw a gentleman who appeared to be a delivery driver for a local water company carrying two five-gallon water bottles on his shoulders in the 115-degree heat of the Arizona summer. I couldn't help but ask him, "What are you doing? You must make incredible money to be torturing yourself that way!" I kind of laughed when I said it so that he would know I was just playing around, but my point was that he was literally doing a backbreaking job in 115 degrees so he must be getting paid really well.

He responded by telling me that he was not making nearly enough and that he had a second job to make ends meet. Needless to say, I continued the conversation and gave him my card. He and his fiancé came to a presentation about a week later and became two of my best associates. They went on to assume leadership roles within the company and became very successful.

PCM works well because once you are comfortable with talking to people, you have an endless supply of free leads. The best part is that you get choose whom you speak with.

FLYERS

Another way to advertise your business for very little money is to use flyers. I built my business on flyers for the first several months because it was simple, it worked, and it was inexpensive. One of the great things about flyers is that because they are so simple and economical, people realize they can duplicate this form of advertising. Quite frankly, flyers are one of the most effective and predictable forms of advertising you can do. When you're using flyers, there are some things to consider before you get started. If you're going to get the most out of your flyers, you must first have a good master flyer. I have included a few examples of flyers I have used.

When you design your master flyer, it should be simple and effective. Here is my general rule of thumb for designing flyers, as well as some other types of ads: the smallest number of words that will inspire someone to call you is what you want to put in the ad. When you design a flyer or any other type of ad, your objective is not to try to explain the business in the ad. Your objective is simply to get someone to call your 800 number. That's all.

You do not have to spend big money to have your flyers designed professionally. You can do this, but it's not required. I have almost always designed my own flyers and had them printed at a local office supply store. In order to maximize your flyer budget, I suggest having your flyers sized to fit eight or ten on an 8 ½ x 11 sheet. In addition to giving you the most flyers for your dollar, it also gives you a flyer that is a very convenient size. Flyers do not have to be big to work. In fact, in my experience, the smaller the flyer, the better the results. I have even used business card-sized flyers, which work very well. What do you put on a business card-sized flyer? Good question. How about something like this:

This card is worth $400,000 + per year.

Let me show you how.

800-555-0000

Do you think that might raise someone's curiosity? Business card-sized flyers are perfect to keep in your wallet or purse. When you frequent places like restaurants, shopping malls, gas stations, virtually any place, leave one on a counter or table where someone else is sure to see it.

After you've got your flyer designed the way you want it, take the master to someplace like Kinko's or Office Max and have them put the flyer on some card stock, again, eight or ten on a page. I prefer a solar yellow card stock for its visibility, but you can choose another color. Some people prefer green, as green represents money. Color is mostly a matter of personal preference.

When you place the order for your flyers, make sure you tell them to cut the flyers. When you're getting several thousand flyers printed up, you don't want to be sitting there with scissors trying to cut flyers when you should be out distributing them. Most places will charge you an additional dollar amount for each cut. It's worth it.

Now that you know how and where to get your flyers printed, let's talk about where to distribute them. As a general rule, I believe there is almost no bad place to put a flyer. Still, you must use some common sense. The only place I will not distribute flyers is the low-income areas of town. The reason is, while distributing flyers in a low-income area will still generate around a one-percent response rate, that one percent will not likely be qualified for your time. Depending on which company you are with and the product or service you are marketing, some people will not have the means to get involved with your company or product. Outside of that, there is really no bad place to put a flyer.

Some words of caution: some places might have signs that say "No Soliciting" or "No Handbills" or even "No Trespassing." If you see a sign like this, keep in mind that if you proceed with distributing flyers, you are doing so at your own risk of being fined or possibly even incarcerated. Have I ever seen this happen? No, but I must tell you that it is possible. So don't ever try the line, "Oh, Steve said in his book that it was okay to do this." I don't think the cop is going to buy it. Also, you may be asked to pick up the flyers you just distributed. I personally will not do this. I will politely say, "I'm sorry, but this is what I do for a living. I will be happy to stop distributing and leave your property, but I cannot pick up those flyers." At that point I turn and leave the property. I don't wait around to see if they are going to call the police.

When you are distributing flyers in parking lots, first of all, pick the biggest parking lots you can find. I prefer shopping centers and strip malls as well as sporting events. These will make you more efficient with your time. Second, when you put flyers on cars, do not put them on the windshield. This just makes people angry. If they get in their car and don't see the flyer until after they are already driving, they must stop and get out of the car to get that darn thing off the windshield. I can almost promise you they will not be receptive to your opportunity. If you're going to put flyers on cars, put them in between the driver's side door and the glass, just above the door handle. This way the person sees it when they reach for the door handle. If it won't go in that spot or won't stay, skip the vehicle. Also, *do not* throw the flyer into the car if the window is open. People will feel like their space has been violated.

Remember, when you're distributing flyers, it's a numbers game. You're going to see around a one percent response, so that tells you that if you expect to talk to fifty people, you had better put out at least five thousand flyers. If you think putting out a couple hundred flyers will work, think again. In my opinion, you should not distribute fewer than one thousand flyers each time you go out. If you are distributing flyers in large parking lots, one thousand flyers should take between two and three hours and that's if you are working alone. You can cut that time in half by getting a friend to help you.

FLYER COMPANIES

Companies exist that will print, cut, and distribute your flyers for you. I recommend that you research these companies before ordering their service. Make sure there is a way to track your flyer or that the company has a "proof of delivery" system in place so that you know your flyers are going out. Companies like this and their services range in price, so check your local area for details.

Door hangers are another type of flyer you can do. Many types of businesses like cable companies, pizza deliveries, restaurants, and landscaping companies use door hangers. Door hangers produce around the same one percent response that flyers receive. If you are going to use door hangers, I suggest letting that company distribute them for you. Distributing flyers door-to-door is not time efficient and it takes forever.

Remember this: if you are going to do flyers, you must go into it knowing it is a numbers game. You are going to get chased off parking lots, you are going to be asked to leave properties, and you will also be asked to pick up the flyers you have just distributed. It is not glamorous work, but if you are looking for predictable response rates and are working with little or no advertising budget, flyers are an excellent means to generate leads.

More Sample Flyers

Fire Your Boss!

Learn to Earn Six Figures
from Home.

Call

800-555-0000

Are You Tired of Making
Someone Else Rich?

Become self-employed and learn to
earn six figures from home.

800-555-0000

Classified Ads

Another place to advertise is in the classified section of a local paper. If you're going to use classified ads to generate leads, there are some things you'll want to know before you get started. The first thing is how to write a good ad. Again, like flyers, classified ads should be short and simple. The smallest number of words you can put in the ad that will entice someone to pick up the phone and call the number is what you want. You're not trying to explain anything in the ad. The objective is not to sell the person on your product or service but simply to get them to call your number.

When you're writing a classified ad, make sure the ad starts with the letter A or B. This will ensure the ad is at the beginning of the section you are running it in. Sometimes numbers and symbols are placed before the letters of the alphabet. Check with the paper you want to run your ad in. Here is one of my favorite classified ads:

> ### A $400,000 first-year income potential.
> # 800-555-0000.

No fluff, no explaining, but it definitely raises curiosity.

Now that you've got your ad, here are some tips on how to maximize your classified ad dollar. When you call the publication you are going to run your ad in, tell them you are an in-house agent. This will almost always get you a lower rate than you would normally get otherwise. Another way to lower the cost of advertising is to place the ad for several weeks at a time. The more weeks you buy, the more economical the ad will be. Leaving the ad in for a long period will produce better results than if you just leave it in for one or two weeks. My suggestion is to put the ad in and forget it.

If you want to run in more than one publication or maybe you just don't know which publication you would like to run your ad in, you can find an excellent resource at the local library. The *Gayle Media Guide* is a directory of publications and broadcast media. In this guide you can access information on publications all over the country, including demographics, circulation, etc. This is an excellent resource tool if you plan on using classified ads or print ads. You can also work with brokers to place your ad in hundreds of papers at the same time. This is much more economical than placing an ad in one paper at a time. For more information on newspaper brokers or ad brokers, look them up on your favorite search engine. You can typically run an ad through a broker in several hundred papers for a couple hundred bucks.

Some types of publications to consider for classified advertising can be major local publications, small town publications, civic organization publications, industry publications, alternate lifestyle publications, religious publications, and common interest (hobby) publications. These are just a few of the different types of publications you can advertise in.

Fax Advertising

Before I talk about fax advertising, or "fax blasting," I want to make it very clear there is a federal law on the books that prohibits sending unsolicited faxes. *Doing this is against the law.* I will tell you as well that apparently many people have not gotten the memo yet. I still get unsolicited faxes on my fax machine every day. Since it is an option for you to choose or not to choose, I am going to include this section with the understanding that sending <u>unsolicited</u> faxes is against the law. If you choose to do it, it is at your own risk of legal action.

Fax advertising is a form of advertising that is about as simple as you can get. It is not only simple, it is effective. I'm sure everyone has seen fax ads come across their fax machine at one time or another. I always ask myself, "Where did this come from and how did they get my fax number?"

Here is how fax blasting works. A company generates a database of fax numbers. These numbers can come from any number of sources. As the fax numbers are accumulated in the database, the company can sell fax advertising to those numbers. Let's say you want to do some fax advertising. You call the fax advertising company and tell them you want to send out 50,000 fax ads. They will then fax your flyer or ad to 50,000 numbers from their database. To respond to your ad, which has a return fax number or an 800 voicemail number in it, people fax their information back to you or call your 800 number. Simple.

With fax advertising, you can expect anywhere from a fraction of a percent return to a several percent return. A good target is one percent. You can generally find fax blast companies in the phone book or on your favorite search engine. A word of caution: do some checking on the company before you give them your money. Less than reputable companies have ripped off more than one person.

Magazine Ads

When you feel like you are generating a fairly substantial income and you would like to step up the advertising, magazines are an option. Because there are so many different types of magazine publications, you can target virtually any market you wish very easily.

The way to start a magazine ad is simply to get a copy of the magazine you want to advertise in and flip to about the second or third page where it lists all the names of the people on the staff of that publication. Skim down through the departments till you come to advertising. There will be the name or names of the person or persons in charge of advertising. Call the publication and ask for that person and they will tell you what you need to get started. You will generally have to provide your own artwork for the ad, but most publications will be able to refer you to someone if you don't have your artwork already.

Some things to consider before running a magazine ad: first, magazine ads are typically going to have a higher fee for service than classifieds or newspapers. Second, while magazine ads are slower producers than some of the other forms of advertising, they are generally excellent leads, though this varies depending on what publication your ad is running in. My personal opinion is, if you've got the money to spend on magazine ads, go with the biggest color ad you can afford and leave it in for at least three months. Magazine ads are typically great producers because you have more perceived credibility when you advertise in a magazine. People tend to feel that if you have the money to advertise in the magazine, you must be making some money with your opportunity. I recommend running at least a half-page, full-color ad, though I typically run full-page, full-color ads in magazines.

OTHER ADVERTISING METHODS

There are too many advertising mediums to list them all here, but I would like to cover just a few. In case you have been asleep or off the planet for the past fifteen years, there is this new thing out now called the Internet. In my opinion, this is one of the most important advancements within the past century and is a great place to advertise your business. You do not have to be a rocket scientist to do it, either. If you go to your favorite search engine and type in "On-Line Advertising," you will be bombarded with places to advertise. Some have fees and some do not. There are hundreds of places to advertise on the Internet for little or no money at all. This is just one more lead generation source for you to use.

As you drive around town, you will likely see vehicles with window advertising or stick-on signs promoting a particular business. Window advertising, if done well, is not out of the question, but I do not recommend it. You will be able to see why in the following example.

Years ago when I first got started, I was doing my best to come up with a creative and economical way to advertise. The trouble was, while I was attempting to be creative, I was also doing a very good job of re-inventing the wheel. I decided that I would put magnetic signs on the side of my vehicle. Great idea, right? Wrong. Considering that my vehicle was a $500 beat-up Chevy Astro Van, this was not the best idea. Since I didn't have the money to have the signs professionally produced, I decided to go to the local hardware store and buy $7 magnetic sign kits. It seemed like a great idea at the time.

I took the sign kits home and spent a couple of hours working on my signs so they would be perfect. The white magnetic bases with black letters were going to look so good on the side of my van! This is how the signs read:

Work from Home

Earn $3,000 -$5,000/Week

Let me show you how.

888-555-0000

I hurried out to the van to apply each of the signs so that I could go drive around, knowing the calls were going to come pouring in. I jumped in the van and bolted out into the Atlanta afternoon rush hour. I intentionally drove head-on into five o'clock gridlock with absolutely no fear. Considering how much I dislike traffic, you can guess how excited I was.

After a couple of hours of exposing my new signs of opportunity, I drove home with anticipation, knowing the messages would already be waiting. When I got home I was astonished to find that there were exactly zero calls and zero messages. After further evaluation of my great advertising plan, I came to realize that it actually didn't make a whole lot of sense. "Earn $3,000-$5,000/Week" on the side of a beat-up Astro van? No wonder nobody called.

The point is, if you drive a beater, don't advertise your business on it. If you drive an E55 Mercedes or a BMW or something at the opposite end of the spectrum, you probably are not going to want to stick signs on it anyway. Your success is already evident.

CO-OP ADVERTISING

If you really want to do some bigger ticket advertising but maybe you don't quite have the big-ticket budget, you may want to participate in an advertising co-op. Co-op advertising is a way to get into those higher-end forms of advertising and still keep the fees reasonable.

The way a co-op works is, several people typically share the fees of the ad and then split the leads equally amongst the group. I will generally set up a separate 800 voicemail for the co-op and add an extension for each person participating in the ad. As the calls come into the 800 number, each message goes into the next voicemail box in the rotation. The leads are split evenly so that no person can cherry pick the good leads. Some common co-op ads are billboards, mobile billboards, magazines, radio spots, television spots, national news publications, etc.

Co-op advertising on a radio ad might have a fee of $5,000 for the week, depending on several factors. If you put ten people in the co-op to share the leads, each person puts in $500 and everyone still benefits from the ad.

CHAPTER 4 SUMMARY

*G*etting started in network marketing can be a very rewarding experience, provided you have done some research and have selected a good company with a product or service you feel good about. Remember, some companies have given the industry a black eye because of their unethical practices, so you must do your homework.

- Research companies thoroughly before becoming an associate. Check with local state and federal agencies to affirm that there are no challenges with the company you are interested in or its principals.
- Shop for your advisor. Provided it does not cause problems, look for the person you would like to be mentored by before you get started. Once you enroll, it is most likely too late.
- Develop a clear, concise plan. Spend some time with your advisor or sponsor so you can map out exactly what your plan is to get started and become successful.
- Purchasing leads is a great way to supplement your primary lead generation sources, but make sure you do some research on the lead company before you send them any money.

continued

- Utilize an 800 voicemail number. If your company does not have a 800 voicemail as part of your back office, make sure you get one set up on your own. 800 voicemail service is a powerful tool for your business.
- Always have business cards. They are a sign of professionalism and are a powerful tool for networking and personal contact marketing.
- Training events will shorten your learning curve and they are how the top income earners got to be top income earners. Attending all of the local, regional, and national training events is the best way to learn from those who have already done it and to catch their enthusiasm.

Chapter 5

Retailing Your Product or Service

Network marketing has come a long way over the past twenty to thirty years. Today there are literally hundreds of opportunities to get involved with. When I was about six or seven years old, my mother was involved with a few different companies. Each was product-based and my mother was very successful. She sold Kirby vacuum cleaners, Shaklee, and Avon. These were just a few of the previous generation network marketing companies.

Today, we not only have product-based companies, we also have service-based companies. In my opinion, one of the reasons some of the older companies such as Amway, now called Quixtar, are still around is that they are heavily based on retail sales. Unfortunately, many companies have attempted to duplicate the power of these types of compensation plans without actually having a tangible product or service. Most of those who tried have failed. Without a retailible product or service, the company is essentially a money game, which the attorney general tends to frown on. My point is, having a product or service you are able to sell retail is like having a whole separate income stream.

Many people do not even participate in the income opportunity part of their company because of the large amount of income they generate simply retailing their products and services. There are several ways to retail a product that can be very profitable. Below I cover a few of those ways.

Kiosks

Renting a kiosk at a mall or department store can be a very profitable way to retail your product. The primary advantage is traffic exposure. Depending on the location and the season, your product or service can be exposed to tens of thousands of people each week. Another advantage is that you do not have to chase down leads. The prospects come right to you. Kiosks are not expensive, and if this fits your situation, a kiosk sales center could increase your results substantially.

Product Expos

If you have ever been to a large product expo or convention, you have seen the large convention hall setting with hundreds of booths set up in rows so that customers can literally shop a smorgasbord of products. There is a reason these events are booked more than a year in advance in most cases. Vendors know the selling power they have when they have a booth at these types of conventions.

Similar to kiosks, a product expo has customers coming right to you from the minute the doors open until the minute they close, and you never have to leave your booth. The difference between a kiosk and a product expo is primarily time and traffic. A product expo will only last a matter of days in most cases and will generate as much as ten times the traffic as a kiosk.

SPONSORSHIPS

Being successful in retailing requires that you think outside the box. How creative can you be? Sponsorships are a way to generate retail sales. You can sponsor sporting events, athletes, teams, racecars, grand openings, ribbon-cuttings, social events, contests, telethons, print publications, radio and TV programs, animals, people in events, and the list goes on and on. A sponsorship gets your product exposure to the public. Which of these ideas would work for your product or service?

FREE SEMINARS

One of the most powerful ways to retail a product or service is to do a free seminar. The way a free seminar typically works is, first, you decide on a date and venue for your seminar. Once this information is determined, ideally six to eight weeks out, you start promoting your free event. How you promote is up to you. I suggest printing admission tickets and acquiring a mailing list from within your product industry and sending two free tickets to each name.

I also recommend running ads on morning and afternoon drive-time radio. If your budget permits, run some half or full-page ads in the local papers. Advertise in as many places as you can for the six to eight weeks leading up to the event. As the event gets closer, pump up the excitement with some hype in the ads. Let people know there are only six days left to get their tickets to this event.

On the day of the event, bring in a speaker or perhaps do the seminar yourself. Either way, a speaker gets up and does a three- to six-hour seminar on something having do with your product. It should not be about your product directly, but something to do with your product, either a related service or benefit, or maybe about the industry your product is in.

At the end of the seminar, the speaker closes with, "By the way, if you liked what you saw here today, this product/service is available from the folks in the back of the room as you leave." I watched a group of ten people do a co-op for an event just like this and in three days they generated $150,000 and made $100,000 profit. Just think how wonderful it would be to do that once a month.

Seven Steps of the Sales Process

When I was marketing, I spent a considerable amount of time reading personal development books and listening to audio programs. I believe this is one of the primary reasons I am where I am today. One of the authors I read and studied was Tom Hopkins, author of *The Builder of Sales Champions*. I figured that if I were in a direct sales business, I had better know how to sell. Tom's material taught me not only how to be a better sales professional but also how to build solid relationships in business. Since that time, I've had the opportunity to market Tom's one-day seminar, which taught me even more.

One thing I feel many people in network marketing are missing when they first get started is the concept of the sales process and how it works. Tom Hopkins teaches what he calls the "Seven Steps of the Sales Process," and he truly breaks down each of the seven steps in order to help a person understand the importance of each one and the details involved in each. I am not going to go into detail about each of the seven steps, but I would like to give you the steps so you can see the whole process.

Step 1: Prospecting. Where are your leads coming from?

Step 2: Original Contact. This is your chance to build rapport.

Step 3: Qualification. Is the client qualified? What does the client have now? What does the client enjoy about what he or she has now? What would the client alter about what he or she has now? Who is the decision-maker? What is the best solution for the client?

Step 4: Presentation. How is your presentation? Pre-plan it, practice it, perfect it, and perform it.

Step 5: Handling Areas of Concern. Can you overcome objections in order to move on to the close?

Step 6: Closing. Most people know one or two closes. How many do you know?

Step 7: Follow Up. Get those referrals.

CHAPTER 5 SUMMARY

$\mathcal{M}$any successful companies such as Avon and Amway, now called Quixtar, are heavily based on retail sales. Unfortunately, other companies have attempted to duplicate the power of these types of compensation plans without actually having a tangible product or service. Most of those who have tried have failed. Without a retailible product or service, the company is essentially a money game. Having the ability to retail a product or service in addition to building your team is like having a whole separate income stream. There are many ways to retail a product or service:

- Referrals. Asking your existing customers and clients for referrals will generate retail sales.
- Kiosks. Rent a kiosk at the local mall or shopping center. This allows you to capitalize on all the passing foot traffic.
- Product Expos. Rent a booth at a product or business expo. Again, capitalize on foot traffic.
- Sponsorships. Sponsor a festival or recreational event in your local area.
- Free Seminars. Scheduling a free seminar and then offering your product or service at the end of the event can generate hundreds of sales in just a few hours.
- Seven Steps of the Sales Process. One thing I feel many

continued

people in network marketing are missing
when they first get started is the concept of the sales
process and how it works:

    Prospecting

    Original Contact

    Qualification

    Presentation

    Overcoming Objections

    Closing

    Follow Up

CHAPTER 6

Prospecting with Posture

KEYS TO EFFECTIVE PROSPECTING

*P*rospecting is the heart of your business. The fact is, if you're not prospecting, you're not making money, and if you're not making money, you're not prospecting. Prospecting is absolutely essential if you want to earn a substantial income. However, before you pick up the phone, I recommend taking care of some important preparation tasks.

First of all, have plenty of leads. You cannot prospect effectively if you're in what is referred to as "lead poverty." If you do not have a stack of leads on your desk when you sit down to prospect, you will be clinging to the leads you do have and consequently displaying need to the person you're talking to. Only around fifty percent of prospects will qualify for your time when you're prospecting correctly. If you're in lead poverty, you will attempt to mold each person into the type of person you're looking for, thereby showing need. On the other hand, if you have plenty of leads, you can sort right through them and only take the ones that are truly qualified. We'll discuss more on qualifying in the next section.

In addition to having plenty of leads, you must have a suitable area to work in. By that I mean having an area that's set up in a way that is conducive to being productive for you. I suggest having a desk or similar work area and a comfortable chair where you can manage your business properly. If you have bills on your desk, put them away somewhere out of sight. The last thing you want to be thinking about when you are prospecting is the stack of bills you have to pay. If you don't have a headset phone, get one. This is one of the most important parts of prospecting. If you are using a headset phone to prospect, you will be more comfortable and more productive. It will also leave your hands free to gesture with, as well as give you the ability to take notes while you're prospecting.

Next, get your mindset right. If you've had a bad day, don't jump on the phone and try to prospect. Whatever has made your day bad is going to come through in your voice and kill your prospecting results. Do whatever you have to to get your mindset in the right place, whether it's listening to music or personal development material, doing yoga, or meditating. Whatever it is, do it. If your mindset is not right when you start prospecting, you will not have any success.

The next thing you need is a good system in place to record information from each prospect. When I prospect, I have a log with the person's name, phone number, date and time that they called, a 1–10 score of their message, a place for my notes when I call them back, and the outcome of the call, such as whether or not I booked them for a presentation.

Name	Phone	Date/Time	Score	Notes	Booked

The great thing about prospecting over the phone is that people can't see you. You can be whoever and whatever you want. If you are new in network marketing and haven't made one sale or enrolled one person yet, that's okay. The person you are talking to does not know that, and it is not necessary for them to know. I'm not suggesting you be dishonest, but if you follow my advice, you won't have to worry because they will think they are talking to the top income earner.

The key to effective prospecting is to act "as if." In other words, act "as if" you are the top income earner. Again, do not lie, but be yourself as that person. Go back to the visualization exercise we did earlier. Imagine yourself as the perfect leader, the top income earner, and build yourself up to be that in your mind. Get that image and see it clearly. Listen to how you will sound when you are talking to your prospect. Once you have this in your mind and you feel you can be that leader, it is time to pick up the phone and begin prospecting.

There are a couple of things that will help you in your telephone prospecting. First, make sure you are confident. You must have the posture and tone of a very successful person. If you don't, your prospects will hear it in your voice and they will either hang up or ask you, "Well, how much money have you made?"

If you just got started in your business, this is the last question you want to answer. If you do get that question, I recommend handling it this way, with posture and without any hesitation. Say, "I just got started so I haven't made anything yet, but I know I'm on track to make a strong six-figure income this year. More importantly, how much do you want to make?" If you handle the question like this, you will have far better results than if you hesitate or stutter in your answer.

Second, know what you are going to say. Most companies have prospecting scripts. I recommend using scripts to help you become proficient at what you are going to say, but only for that. If you prospect while you are reading the script, people are going to hear it. If you do not know the script, do not begin prospecting. Instead, practice, practice, practice! It shouldn't take more than a day or two to learn the script, and then you can begin prospecting. People can tell if you are using a script. If they realize you are using one, you will lose all credibility and will likely lose the chance to enroll the person.

For this reason, I strongly recommend that you learn your script as quickly as possible. Practice for as long as it takes until you can do the script in a normal conversational tone.

You should be able to go through your script without any-one knowing it's a script. The way you do that is by using your voice the way you do when you are talking to someone in a normal conversation.

When you talk normally, your voice fluctuates in tone and volume with emphasis on certain words. You must be able to do that with your script. Practice your script until you can do it naturally. You'll know you've got it down when you can improvise and adapt to the person you are talking to and the conversation as required. Not every prospecting call is going to go the same way. You are going to speak to people with strong postures as well as people with weak and timid postures. You must be able to adapt to each of them without reading.

Using the Script

The most important part of using the script during prospecting, and possibly the most difficult, is not sounding like you're reading from a script. I cannot stress enough that if you have to read the script when you prospect, you will have very little success because people will be able to tell you are reading and they will not believe what you are telling them.

The best way to eliminate this challenge, in my opinion, is to actually memorize the script. That means you can recite the script without looking at it. This will enable you to talk to your prospect in a normal conversational tone without sounding like you're reading. It will also allow you to make adjustments in the script, if necessary, to fit the particular personality of the person you're talking to. This might be something as simple as just changing your tone or the speed at which you're speaking. In some cases, you may have to add or omit a word or sentence. The key is to match the tone and speed of the person you are dealing with.

After you have learned the script, you will want to make sure you have a pen and paper handy so you can make notes as you go through the script. What you will be making notes of are what I call "hot buttons." Hot buttons are the person's answers to the questions you ask in the script. These questions are very important. Listen carefully when you ask the questions, because the person is going to tell you exactly why they should get started in your business. By the way, these are the same questions I have used for several years.

Before you start in on the questions from your script, it is very important to first ask the prospect, *"Have I caught you at a good time?"* Out of respect for their time, do not launch off into your script without asking. This could be the difference in thousands of dollars for you.

> ■ The first question is, *"What are you doing for a living right now?"* Right away, you'll have a pretty good idea of what kind of income and even lifestyle the person may be accustomed to. The follow-up questions to this are important as well.
> ✔ *"Great, how long have you been doing that?"* This will tell you a little about stability. If the person is working at a convenience store and has been there for one week, this is a good indication he or she may not be qualified for your time.

- ✔ The last follow-up to the first question is, *"How's that going for you?"*
  Many times this will tell you why the person is looking for something other than what they are doing. For example, they might say, "Oh, it's okay, but my boss is a jerk. I don't make enough money, and right now I'm using the bus to get to work because I have to pay $1,400 to get my car fixed."

- ✔ That will lead you right into the next question, which you will *ask if you* are not sure of the person's answer from the last part of question one: *"What's the main reason you're looking for a business of your own?* Make sure you write this answer down. This is possibly the most important of all of the questions. The answer will be the person's hot button.

- ■ The third question is, *"What kind of income are you accustomed to right now?"* This will tell you whether or not the person might be in a position to come up with the start-up cost. I try never to qualify on money alone if possible, but sometimes it's a must. If a person tells you they only make $1,200 per month, you're going to want to ask the money question at the end. I'll cover that shortly.

- ■ The last question is, *"More importantly, John, what kind of income would you like to generate?"* When you ask this question, make sure the person understands what you're asking. Most people will not tell you their ideal income unless you spell it out for them. For that reason, I like to spell it out. For example: *"Now, John, I want you to think about this for a second before you answer. I don't want to know what's realistic or what would get you by, or what would be okay for starters. I want to know, <u>what would be your ideal income?</u>"* I'm looking for someone who wants to generate at least a six-figure income. That will show me they have vision and desire.

- **The Money Question**—*"John, if I could show you a system that would allow you to achieve the income that you've just told me you are looking for, and you could see without any doubt in your mind that you could do it— John, would it be possible to come up with about $_____ to get your business off the ground?"* (Insert the amount of your product or service plus any additional fees.)

At this point, many of you may be asking, *"How do I get people down to a presentation or a conference call if I haven't made any money yet?"* This is a very good question. I will tell you exactly how you do that even if you haven't made a dime. The best part is, you don't have to lie about your income to do it.

The key to keeping control of the conversation is your posture. Now, obviously, I'm not referring to the way you sit or stand. By posture, I'm referring to the way you present yourself and the confidence you have in your voice when you talk to a prospect.

The question I get from associates possibly more than any other is, "What do I say if someone asks me how much money I've made?" *Again, if you get this question from your prospect, it's a direct indication you do not have the correct posture when you're prospecting. If this is happening to you, get on the phone with your advisor and let him or her help you adjust your posture. At the same time, if you do get that question from a prospect, don't just hang up on them and immediately call your advisor. The way to handle it is to simply say,* "You know what, I just got started and I haven't made a dime yet, but I know for a fact I'm right on track to generate a multiple six-figure income in the next year."

If a prospect asks you how much money you have made, it is vitally important that you not hesitate with your answer. If you hesitate, stumble, or stutter, you have just lost that prospect. If you answer with confidence in your voice and don't hesitate, that person will be far more likely to show up at the presentation.

Maintaining control of the conversation in this manner will also help eliminate the prospect badgering you with questions. Another way to help reduce the number of questions is to shorten the pauses between sentences. This does not mean you should talk faster. Simply shorten the amount of time you pause between each sentence. This will reduce the chance of someone interjecting a question. You're always going to have people who interrupt you to ask questions, but remember, this is an indication the person is not coachable and trainable.

You can refer to the Prospecting Call FAQ's in Appendix D at the back of the book for ways to handle the most common questions. Again, you can also monitor your posture and confidence by the number of questions you get from the prospect. When you listen to leaders prospect, rarely do you hear them get any questions at all from prospects. When you do, the questions are generally derailed immediately. I rarely received questions while prospecting, and was almost never asked, *"How much money do you make?"* Your posture, tone, and confidence are key to effective prospecting.

Qualifying Your Prospects

In network marketing, the key is numbers. The more people you speak with, the better your results are going to be. The challenge with increasing your numbers to increase your results is that the number of tire-kickers and time-wasters also goes up. What you must do is have a system for qualifying prospects so that you can reduce the number of time-wasters to a minimum, thereby further increasing your result. The way to do this is through a process called qualifying.

Qualifying is simply a way to set standard values of acceptance for the questions you ask a prospect. You can set them however you like, but I recommend setting them high enough so that you make sure to eliminate those who will not have the financial means to get started.

In order for someone to qualify for my time, they must have the desire to generate at least $100,000 within the next twelve months, no exceptions. This is not to say that making $85,000 is not respectable, but I have to draw the line somewhere. The more success you have in this business, the more valuable your time will become, and it will not be worth your time to work with people who don't have a sincere desire to generate at least six figures.

The second part of qualifying for my time is being coachable and trainable. If someone is not coachable and trainable, I will not work with them. Such individuals will insist on re-inventing the wheel and doing things their own way without listening to the people who have had success before them. When I talk to prospects, my goal is simply to find out whether or not they are qualified for my time. If they are, I either invite them to a business presentation or arrange a live or recorded presentation call to take them to so they can get the information they need and get their questions answered.

The way I find out if someone is qualified or not is to take them through a very simple script and ask them some key questions. As I'm doing this, I take notes on their answers and also listen for any sign that they are not the person I want to work with. If I find anything that lets me know they are not qualified for my time, I immediately let them go. I will not waste my time trying to change them into someone I want to work with. This is a waste of my time and shows the person that I need them, and I don't *need* anyone to come into my business. Remember that if you have to drag someone into your business, you will have to drag him or her to work as well.

Some keys that let you know someone is not qualified for your time are when this person continually interrupts you, badgers you with questions, says, "I'm not coming down to any meeting unless you can tell me what this is all about," or does not have the desire to generate at least six figures.

THREE-WAY SUPPORT

Another important component of prospecting with posture is using three-way support. In this business, it can be crucial to your success. A three-way call is generally used on a follow-up call, but you should use three-way support anytime the situation dictates. A three-way call occurs when you utilize another associate for third-party validation, edification, or to answer questions a prospect may have on a follow-up call. Three-way calls benefit you in a couple of ways.

First, if you're a new associate and are not comfortable answering questions on a follow-up call, another associate can help out. Second, three-way calls demonstrate to the prospect the level of support they can expect with this company.

When you use a three-way support call, it is very important that you do it correctly. The way a three-way is conducted is actually very simple. The first thing you're going to do when a prospect asks you a question on a follow-up call is say, "You know, John, that's a great question. Can you hang on a second while I get someone on the line who can answer that for you?"

Then you hit your flash button and start dialing. Call someone you know can answer that person's question. You may not get that person on the first try, but don't ever click back to the prospect until you've reached someone who has agreed to do your three-way. When the person says they can do the three-way, tell them a little about the prospect and what his or her question is. At that point, you can click back over to the prospect and introduce the two.

When you do an introduction, you should always edify the person you have brought on the line and then introduce the advisor or associate first. It should sound something like this: "John, I've taken the liberty of bringing Doug Smith on the line. Doug is one of the top income earners in the company as well as a fantastic leader. He's helped me tremendously in building my business. John, this is Doug. Doug, this is John."

At this point, pull out some scissors and cut a six-inch piece of duct tape and apply it directly to your lips. In other words, sit back and *shut up*! I cannot stress this enough. Once you've done the introduction, do not say another word. If you do, you will destroy all the credibility you have just given to that person. When the call is over, you shouldn't have to say much more than goodbye.

Many companies use three-way support and most likely have a list of people who are available to call and the times they are available.

MASSIVE ACTION EQUALS MASSIVE RESULTS

As you work your business, remember that it's a numbers game. Regardless of whether you're doing flyers or faxes or any other form of advertising, the more people you get your ad in front of, the better the results you're going to have. If you're doing flyers, don't go out and do a couple of hundred flyers and sit back and complain that you're not making any money. As I stated earlier, you will see around a one percent response rate on flyers. If you want to make three sales each week, here is what you should expect to do: the fifty percent rule means that to make three sales each week, I need between seven and ten people at a presentation or on a presentation call each week. In order to have seven to ten people at a presentation, I should expect to invite fourteen to twenty people. Show rates are going to vary from associate to associate, but if you can maintain a fifty percent show rate, you are doing very well. Typically, if I book fifteen people, I can expect seven of them to show up. Out of the seven who show, I can expect three to four to get started.

If you are not experiencing results somewhere close to this, chances are you are not qualifying your prospects properly. I suggest getting on the phone with your advisor and finding out where improvements can be made.

Training and Events

As I stated earlier, training and the training events in this business are crucial to your success. There is not a half-way manner in which to do this business. If you are clinging to your job while you work your business because you are afraid of losing your security if this doesn't work, you are planning to fail. In my opinion, there is only one way to do this business, and that is with the one hundred percent belief that you are successful.

Notice I didn't say you "will be" successful? Go into this with the mindset that you *are* successful. The way to instill that belief in yourself and keep it is to utilize all the training events as well as the techniques outlined in this book.

I learned this from those who went before me, and now I would like to pass it along so that you, too, may rise to the top. Some associates think they can do it better their way and you will recognize them when you see them. Learn from them, as well. Learn how *not* to do things. These are typically the associates who want to re-invent the wheel because they can do it better. They are the associates who do not show up at training events and do not get on training calls. They will, however, complain, make excuses, and blame others for their lack of results. Do not let these associates infect you with their negativity. If you use the resources you have, you will be miles ahead of the rest of the crowd.

This is a very simple business, providing that you don't over-complicate things or try to re-invent it. One of the most important things you can do to build your business is simply to be coachable and trainable. Part of being coachable and trainable is making sure you utilize all the training and support that is available to you to assist in building your business. Training will consist of anything from a weekly team call to regional and national trainings. Your advisor will be able to inform you what events are upcoming. Attending a training or a team call once a month is not sufficiently utilizing the resources that you have available. In order to expect any great amount of success, make sure you attend all the trainings.

Chapter 6 Summary

*P*rospecting is absolutely essential if you want to earn a substantial income. You cannot prospect effectively if you're in what is referred to as "lead poverty." If you do not have a stack of leads on your desk when you sit down to prospect, you will be clinging to the leads you do have and consequently displaying need to the person you're talking to. Here are a few prospecting guidelines:

- Prospecting is mandatory for a successful business. It is impossible to close new business without leads.
- You can be anyone on the telephone. Even if you are brand new in the business, you can have the posture and tone of the top income earner in the company.
- A script is a tool, not a crutch, and it must be internalized. If you read the script, your prospect will be able to hear it in your voice and that will rob your credibility. If you are reading your script, you cannot listen effectively to the prospect.
- Not everyone will qualify for your time. Only a certain percentage of prospects will qualify, so do not attempt to convince them. If you have to drag them in, you will have to drag them to work.
- Do not prospect in "need mode." Your energy will come through and you will not have success.

continued

- Using three-way support gives validation and demonstrates a simple system.
- Massive action equals massive results. Learn to love the word "No." Every "No" gets you one step closer to a "Yes."
- Training events are a key to success. Never miss a training event.

CHAPTER 7

Etiquette for Success

Note: before I launch into this chapter, I am going to give you, as a reader and an associate, a brief disclaimer. You are going to find that this chapter is written with a somewhat stronger tone than the rest of the book. In the time I have been in the network marketing industry, I have had the opportunity to learn from my own mistakes as well as my own successes. I have also been fortunate to learn from watching other associates.

Please understand that there is no feeling in the world like experiencing success in your own business. The first time you close a sale or enroll a new associate, the excitement can sometimes be too much to keep inside. The challenge comes when associates forget to maintain their composure or their professionalism while still in that business environment.

This business can also come with some frustration, which is sometimes difficult to control as well. Whether it's excitement or frustration, both of these emotions, if not kept in check, can cost an associate a sale. I have seen some of the most bizarre behavior in this business. None of what you are going to read in this chapter is intended to be offensive, so please do not take it that way. The information is intended to help you avoid the mistakes that *others and I have made. You can choose to accept it or ignore it. Either way, I wish you success.*

Being an associate in your company can be an extremely rewarding opportunity, not only financially, but personally as well. In order for you to experience these rewards, you need to be aware of a few things. This is not a typical job, which means you will not have a boss or supervisor looking over your shoulder to make sure you are working. The bottom line is, this is your opportunity. Only you can choose how you conduct yourself. Should you stick to the system and work it like a business, it will reward you like a business. If you choose to work it like a hobby, it will cost you money like a hobby.

As an independent associate with your company, the way in which you conduct yourself and your business has a direct reflection on your company. With this in mind, it is important to maintain the highest degree of ethics and proper etiquette in your business so that we may all continue to reap the personal and financial rewards, as well as ensure the longevity of the company. It is for this reason that this chapter was created. This section will identify some of the common etiquette pitfalls that new associates fall into as well as ways to avoid them. As you read, be conscious of the way you conduct yourself in situations similar to those used as examples within this section.

As you may already know, there are several ways in which you can "plug in" to the system your company has in place. You may have access to live presentations, you may be utilizing the live or recorded conference call system, or you may be sending people to the website. However you choose to work, it is important to remember the proper way in which to conduct yourself. Again, this will not only shorten your learning curve, it will also help protect the longevity of your company.

Think of the first time you were introduced to this opportunity. Did the person who introduced you to your company seem professional? Were you comfortable with the way that person conducted him or herself? With that thought in mind, think of what you liked or didn't like about the experience. Each area of this opportunity has certain steps that should be followed to maintain a high level of professionalism. This not only benefits you but also everyone around you, whether it is other associates and advisors or guests of other associates and advisors. Should you be present at a live presentation or on a conference call and do or say something unprofessional that could cost someone else a sale, they will most likely not be very happy with you. So, once again, be aware that your behavior affects everyone around you. Now, with that out of the way, let's get started.

PCM ETIQUETTE

If you've read the chapter on advertising and marketing, you already know that PCM is an effective and fun way to build your income. The best part about PCM is it's free. If you keep in mind that you're simply having fun while doing this, it will make it much easier to stay within the etiquette guidelines. PCM should not come across as pushy or high pressure. The key to PCM is to be authentic with people and have a sincere desire to help them change the quality of their lives. The following are some simple guidelines to follow when doing PCM:

1. As Chapter 4 demonstrates, make sure the introduction of your opportunity comes about naturally. For example, say you're standing in line at the store and the person working the register says, "Oh, I can't wait to get out of here and go home . . . I've worked ten hours today." This would be a great time to hand that person your business card and say something like, "Hey, if you're sick of working these ten-hour days, here's my card. Give me a call. I can help you." Then simply walk away. No pressure. What I do not recommend is initiating the conversation by walking up and saying "Hey, how would you like to work out of your home and make thousands of dollars?" Don't get into high-pressure sales. Let other companies do that stuff.

2. If you talk with someone who is interested in getting more information and they want to ask you questions on the spot, simply let them know that you are in a hurry and they should call you at the number on your card. You will be happy to get them more information if they call. Again, walk away. This does two things. First, it eliminates you having to stand there selling and explaining, and two, it keeps you from appearing needy to the person you are talking with. Have the posture that you are busy and successful. In the case that there

might be someone else in the vicinity who may be evaluating this opportunity, they won't be turned off by something you say or do. Leave everyone with a burning curiosity that gets them to call you.

3. Let's say you run into someone who is complaining about his or her job. You hand them a business care and say, "Here's my card. Give me a call. I can help you." And they come back with, "Oh, yeah, Acme Marketing. I've been talking with John Smith about checking this out." Do you continue to prospect this person? I do not recommend it. If you run into someone who is already talking with another associate or advisor, that person should be off limits. Do not "backdoor" or steal from other associates.

4. Whenever you are marketing by personal contact, make sure you do not mislead the person you are talking with. Do not make promises or in any way guarantee any income. Misleading a prospect not only goes against etiquette, it is also unethical and jeopardizes the company's future. Also, in inviting someone to a live presentation, it is important that they understand that what they will be attending is not an interview. If someone asks, it will be a group presentation. In the event that you should decide to conduct a one-on-one presentation, it is still a presentation and not an interview.

5. One of the great things about PCM is that you can do it at anytime, no matter where you are. In the event that you and another associate approach the same person at the same time, you must keep in mind that if the person you spoke with should decide to get started as a result of the initial conversation, it will be imperative that you both agree whose organization the person will be joining beforehand. Once that decision is made, it is final.

6. When doing PCM, make sure not to disrupt other activities or businesses in the process. If you are speaking with someone who is at work, for instance a server at a restaurant, make sure you are not jeopardizing his or her position. It is not professional to pursue someone while they are in their work environment. If you are in a situation where you believe someone might benefit from your opportunity, keep your contact short so as not to interfere and let that person know to call you for more information. Keeping the contact brief also keeps you from displaying need.

Live Presentation Etiquette

Live presentation etiquette is one of the most important and crucial parts of business etiquette. The way in which you conduct yourself in a live presentation environment has a direct effect on literally everyone's business. The way you present yourself not only makes or breaks your potential sale, it also makes or breaks the sale of any associate who may be around you. It is important that you are always conscious of what you say, your posture, and your tone anytime you are around guests as well as other associates.

When you are a new associate, make sure you pay close attention to the leaders and the way in which they posture themselves in the live presentation environment. One of the best tools available to you as a new associate is the leadership within your company. Watching the leaders and learning how they maintain correct posture throughout the entire marketing process will help you get through your learning curve as quickly as possible. Keep this general rule in mind: the more you listen to the leaders, the faster you will learn. The more you talk, the slower you will learn. It's typically the salespeople who come in and reinvent the wheel who struggle through the learning curve.

Conduct during a live presentation is absolutely crucial to the direction of the entire event. The success of the presentation is directly proportional to the energy of the crowd. The energy of the guests is directly proportional to the energy of the associates and advisors, and all of it will affect the speaker. With this in mind, it is an absolute necessity that you be present for the speaker and have a positive mental and physical posture. Anything that an associate or advisor does that distracts from the presentation is unfair to the speaker and the guests.

Furthermore, it is important to remember that energy is contagious. The energy you put out during a presentation will be received and multiplied by the guests. If your energy is "ho-hum," as in "I've seen this a thousand times," do not expect the guests to be attentive to the speaker. Some of the things that would be considered poor etiquette and are best not seen are listed as follows:

1. Talking during a presentation. Once the presenter takes the floor, please discontinue all conversation and give your attention to the speaker.

2. Playing with electronic devices or other activities that are not associated with the presentation. This includes cell phones, electronic organizers, games, or any other unrelated activities.

3. Leaving the room for anything other than an emergency. Once the presentation begins, stay in your seat. If that means you have to use the restroom before you sit down, do so. Make sure you have gotten a drink of water, your cell phone is turned off, and that you control any overwhelming urges to smoke a cigarette. Leaving the room during a presentation for any reason sends a message to all the guests that it is okay for them to leave as well. This destroys the energy in the room and could be the difference between a sale and a walk-out.

4. Asking questions to prompt coverage of a particular topic. The speaker who handles the presentations knows what information is to be covered. Asking prompting questions undermines the credibility of the presenter and leads to straying questions, which will cause the presentation to get behind schedule.

5. Making or answering phone calls. If your cell phone should happen to ring because you forgot to turn it off, you should immediately turn it off. If for some reason you absolutely must answer your phone, please leave the room before starting the conversation. Talking on a cell phone during a presentation is not only poor etiquette, it is very disrespectful to everyone within the presentation.

6. Having poor body language. Sitting with your arms crossed, not tuning in to the presenter, sleeping, or looking at your watch are all examples of poor body language. Make sure you have good, positive body language.

ELEVATOR ETIQUETTE

"Elevator etiquette" describes how people conduct themselves within the live presentation environment. This name came from watching associates in my company crowd around the elevator door before the start of a live presentation. Each associate was expecting guests at the presentation and wanted to make sure that when his or her guests arrived, they had the opportunity to introduce themselves.

This kind of initiative is great, but as the number of guests and associates continued to grow, there ended up being a huge crowd of associates stampeding every person who walked off the elevator or through the door.

For guests coming to see a business presentation, this can be very scary and quite overwhelming. It is not good etiquette. Generally, the guests are scared away before they have even seen the presentation. Keep the guests and their feelings in mind when at a live presentation.

The proper way to handle this situation is simply to have one or two associates, whatever is necessary, escort guests to the room where the presentation will be held. Chances are, there will be guest information cards for them to fill out when they arrive. The whole purpose of the guest cards is to let you know whether or not your guests attended the presentation. As your organization grows along with everyone else's, the sheer number of guests attending a presentation will make it virtually impossible for you to meet all your guests beforehand. Again, if you take part in the "elevator stampede," it will not only scare your guests, it will scare other people's guests as well.

Pre-Presentation Etiquette

Along the same lines as "elevator etiquette," your professionalism before the start of a presentation is very important to everyone who has guests at the presentation. In the interests of your own business as well as everyone else's, strict adherence to proper etiquette is a must when utilizing live presentations.

For example, it would be poor etiquette to walk into the meeting room prior to the presentation with your list of invited guests in hand and approach each guest saying, "Are you John? Are you here for me?" When you have even a couple of associates going through the room asking each guest who they're here for, it can make your opportunity look like less than a reputable business operation.

As a general rule of thumb, it's best to have the guests brought into the room and seated by one or two associates. If you are expecting guests at the presentation, find a seat and sit quietly until the presentation begins. Either you or your advisor will receive any guest cards from the ushers at the end of the presentation so that you will know exactly how many guests you have in attendance. I don't recommend that you approach the ushers asking if your guests have shown up. As the number of guests in your area increases, it will become impossible for the ushers to keep track of whose guests have checked in.

Light, casual conversation while waiting for the start of the presentation is fine as long as it does not entail any aspects of the business, meaning no shoptalk. Basically, anything that is spoken about regarding business or personal activities, complaints, setbacks, challenges, rumors, questions, or anything not intended for a guest to hear is shoptalk. If you've had a bad week or are experiencing challenges, do not share it with the guests. Use the energy from others to bring your energy up, and do not poison others with your negative energy. There are only two basic guidelines regarding this topic:

1. There should be no shoptalk before, during, or after a presentation.

2. There should be no shoptalk before, during, or after a presentation.

Engaging in shoptalk is a red flag to anyone evaluating your opportunity. If you engage in shoptalk, don't expect anyone to get started.

With that said, any conversation that does occur should be kept to a minimum and at a soft volume, but there should be absolutely no conversation with guests or associates once the presentation begins. If you have had a bad week or are experiencing challenges, do not share it with the guests. Use the energy from others to bring your energy up. Do not poison others with your negative energy. Likewise, any questions or challenges you have should be addressed outside this environment. Remember, this presentation is for the guests.

Finally, on the subject of pre-presentation, it is also recommended that if you are utilizing live presentations to build your business, you should be at all the presentations regardless of whether you have guests scheduled or not. The positive energy will assist you in keeping your mindset positive as well.

Post-Presentation Etiquette

After a presentation is over, it is important to maintain your etiquette and posture as there will be guests who remain to ask further questions. This is when it becomes easy to forget about keeping your posture. If you get so excited about the fact that you have guests staying to get their questions handled that you let your posture and etiquette go out the window, you can very well destroy all the work you have done up to this point and lose the potential sale. What's even worse is if you do something that costs someone else a potential sale.

When a guest or guests stay after a presentation to get their questions answered, make sure you check your posture. Keep the conversation to the questions at hand and avoid chitchat. If you start getting off the subject and making small talk, you will be displaying need. Make sure the guests know you are there to answer their questions and that's all. You have more people to talk to. Keep the posture of someone who is busy and successful. Also, giving guests added information that is not provided by the company is discouraged. If you give them more information to review, you will do two things: first, you will be displaying need, and second, you will overwhelm them. The system works. Do not reinvent the wheel.

If your guest is ready to move forward after the presentation, make sure you schedule a follow-up meeting with them at that time. Ask the person if they have their calendar with them. Make sure you have your calendar as well. This is the best time to lock down a follow-up meeting. Should a guest say they are ready to fill out the paperwork right then, have them go home and sleep on it. You can follow up with them the next day.

THREE-WAY SUPPORT ETIQUETTE

Having good three-way support, also discussed in Chapter 6, is essential for your business. If you are a new associate and are not quite comfortable with answering the most common questions, you should be utilizing three-way support from some of the leaders in the company. Even if you've been doing this for some time, three-way support is a very powerful way to show your prospect the level of support they can expect should they choose to get started.

Three-way support must be done properly. Whether it's over the phone or in person, the procedure is the same. Once you bring in a third person to handle questions from your prospect, inform the prospect who will be handling their questions, introduce that person, and then sit back and be quiet. It is imperative that once you make the introduction you not say another word. If you say anything, you will negate all the creditability you just gave to that person. If the prospect asks you a question directly, answer the question and only that question and then be quiet. This is the procedure whether you are brand new or a top income earner.

Live Conference-Call Etiquette

Live conference calls and live training calls are a major part of this opportunity. Whether you are building your business locally using live presentations or working nationally over the phone, conference calls are a very powerful tool for you to utilize. Because this is such a powerful tool, not only for presentations but for training as well, there can be hundreds of people on a live conference call all at the same time. With this in mind, it is absolutely mandatory that you follow some simple etiquette rules for live conference calls.

1. Make sure you are in a quiet spot for the call. This means no noise whatsoever, not even a little noise. If you can hear it, so can everyone else on the call. Even if it's just a whisper, it can be heard. Make sure you are not shuffling things on your desk, wrestling with the phone, putting dishes away, talking to someone in the room, or doing anything except listening. If your phone does not have a regular mute button, you may want to mute yourself by pressing *6 (star six) or whatever the mute code is with your conference call company. This is only necessary if you don't have a regular mute button and there is a possibility of noise in your background. The host always has the ability to mute the whole system.

2. When you check on a live conference call and you don't hear a host taking introductions, please wait quietly. Do not ask, "Is anyone on?" Sometimes the host or the person taking introductions is not the first one on the call. If you're the first one on the call, just sit quietly and wait. This is not the time to make small talk with other associates or people on the line. *If the host is not on the call, the line should be silent.*

3. Any time you check onto a live conference call or a live training call, make sure you listen to see if someone is still taking introductions or if the call has already begun. If introductions are still being

taken, make sure you let the host know your name and where you are calling from. Do not assume the person taking introductions knows your name or where you are from. There will be people from all over the country on these conference calls, so it's important that you state your name and where you are calling from.

4. I do not recommend three-waying people onto a conference call. This severely degrades the quality of the call. If someone cannot get on the call themselves, they should check with you after the call.

5. If you are on a cell phone, make sure you are able to mute yourself.

6. Pay attention to the host. He or she may be giving information or asking for information that pertains to you. If you are not paying attention and you ask a question that has already been covered, it wastes time for others who would like to be getting their questions answered.

ASSOCIATE RECOGNITION ETIQUETTE

As you build your business, make sure you remember where you came from and why you are doing this. Your associates are the backbone of your organization, and you must do everything possible to assist them in building their own businesses. As your organization grows you will see challenges, as will your associates. When your associates break through these challenges, give them the recognition they deserve. Recognize them on live calls and make sure other people hear their results. The general rule is, "Praise in public and reprimand in private."

ONE-ON-ONE PRESENTATION ETIQUETTE

For those of you who choose to work strictly out of your home or who do not have access to a live presentation, doing one-on-one presentations is a very powerful method of getting information to a prospect. One-on-one's are simple and effective, even if you've just gotten started. The power of a one-on-one comes from the completely authentic and relaxed environment in which you conduct your presentation. If you've just started and haven't made any money yet, that's okay. Don't feel like you can't do a one-on-one presentation if you haven't made any money yet. The most important thing to remember is to be authentic.

As you begin to have success, keep track of your accomplishments as well as your income. You may want to keep copies of your checks for potential customers to look at. This is sometimes a very motivating factor in someone's decision-making process.

There are a few important things to keep in mind when doing one-on-one's. The first is to know what information goes into a presentation. There are some things you can and can't say when doing a presentation. The best way to get all the information on what can and cannot be said is by reading your company's rules and compliance guides or checking with one of the leaders of the company. Also, make sure you are on all the training calls as well as attending the training and regional events.

Another way to become familiar with the process of one-on-one's is to sit in on as many one-on-one's as you possibly can. Check with the leaders in your area to see who is doing one-on-one presentations out of their home or other suitable facility, and ask if you can sit in and observe.

Self-Awareness Etiquette

Your company has people from all over the country as well as people from all kinds of backgrounds. Since some people have never been in situations where they've had to be conscious of how their behavior affects others, it becomes important to maintain a high level of self-awareness so that you do not adversely affect those around you. One of these things to be aware of is your volume control within a business environment. If there are other people working in the area around you, make sure you check your conversational volume so that you are not disturbing others. If necessary, remove yourself from that area in order to continue your conversation or business.

Overall, keep yourself in check so that your level of professionalism is such that you do not hinder anyone else's performance. Remember: what you put out will come back to you tenfold.

CHAPTER 7 SUMMARY

*A*s you may already know, there are several ways in which you can "plug in" to the system that your company has in place. You may have access to live presentations, you may be utilizing the live or recorded conference call system, or you may be sending people to the website. However you have chosen to work, it is important to remember the proper way in which to conduct yourself. Again, this will not only shorten your learning curve, it will also help protect the longevity of your company.

■ Etiquette to remember:
    PCM Etiquette
    Live Presentation Etiquette
    Elevator Etiquette
    Pre-Presentation Etiquette
    Post-Presentation Etiquette
    Three-Way Support Etiquette
    Live Conference-Call Etiquette
    Associate Recognition Etiquette
    One-on-One Etiquette
    Self-Awareness Etiquette

CHAPTER 8

Positioning

The network marketing industry contains many different compensation plans and marketing systems with a variety of different features and benefits. Depending on the company you choose to work with and the compensation plan that is in place, you may have a variety of ways to get your business started. Some companies have different products and service levels that you can take advantage of when you get started. The important thing to consider is, "Am I positioning myself to achieve the maximum result possible in the shortest amount of time?" In order to determine this, look at the compensation plan and see where you must be so that you will generate the most income possible in the shortest amount of time.

If your company has different options for getting started, chances are good that the highest starting position is going to require that you spend a little more money on your business than if you started at the lowest level. This may require that you purchase a certain product or an amount of product in order to do so. It may require that you commit to a certain amount or level of work or service. Either way, you are the one who determines how fast you will start generating income and how much income you will generate. If given a choice, do you want to make a lot or a little? Do you want to make it fast or slow? Positioning gives you the ability to choose.

I suggest looking at it like a business owner and realizing that the total amount to get started at the highest point of almost any company is still far less than the capital outlay for most conventional businesses and franchises. Look at McDonald's. A current McDonald's franchise looks like this:

> **Initial Costs:** $45,000 initial fee paid to McDonald's
>
> **Equipment and Pre-Opening Costs:** Typically, these costs range from $494,750 to $1,030,500. The size of the restaurant facility, area of the country, pre-opening expenses, inventory, selection of kitchen equipment, signage, and style of decor and landscaping will affect new restaurant costs. These costs are paid to suppliers.
>
> ** Information from McDonalds.com*
> *http://www.mcdonalds.com/corp/franchise/purchasingYourFranchise/newRestaurants.html*

When you compare these costs to the fees associated with starting your network marketing business at the top, you will see why it makes sense to start as high as you can. Even if you only make $100,000 your first year, that is considerable compared to the fact that with a franchise you are not going to see a paycheck for three to five years, which means you are working for free. This is the reason home-based businesses are more popular than ever.

Positioning is something that is absolutely key to the amount of time it takes you to have success in your business. Speaking from experience, I can tell you that not positioning yourself as quickly as you possibly can cost you thousands and thousands of dollars. If you have that "Wait and see" attitude, meaning, "I'm not going to position myself until I see if this is really going to work," you will not have success. What you're saying is, "I don't really believe in this, but I'll see what happens."

If you don't believe you'll succeed, guess what? You're absolutely right. If you believe there is absolutely no possible way you can fail, guess what? You're right again. The fact is, this business only works if you believe. With that in mind, it would be foolish to get started and not position yourself as high as possible right off the bat.

I'll share a couple of scenarios with you that are entirely too common. Keep in mind, these are my experiences in a company that had an Australian two-up compensation plan. The first of these was my own experience, a lesson I learned the hard way. I got started in this business when I had literally no money. I had a few things that were worth enough to get started but would have taken too long to liquidate. I made the decision to sell my car in order to come up with the start-up capital. My car wasn't worth enough to get started at the top, but I did manage to come in and get started just below the top. As I started having some success, my advisor kept telling me to position myself at the top or I was going to lose money. I said, "No, I'm not; nobody in my organization is ready to purchase their event ticket yet."

Guess what? I was wrong to the tune of about $24,000. The event ticket was how we referred to the three-day and five-day conferences that were our two top-level products. The three-day event sold for $7,995 and the five-day event sold for $12,995. As a qualified advisor with that company, a person selling the ticket to another associate or a retail customer would make an up-front commission of $5,000 on the three-day event and $8,000 on the five-day event.

It is not hard to see that if someone purchases all three products from you as a qualified advisor, you have had a great day. Now, imagine having two people approach you who both want to purchase all three products at the same time. That is how a person can make $30,000 in one day.

Here is what typically happens: let's say I am an advisor with this network marketing company and we market three products. Our entry-level product sells for $1,495 and has an up-front commission of $1,000. The middle product sells for $7,995 and has an up-front commission of $5,000 paid to the qualified advisor. The top-level product sells for $12,995 and has an up-front commission of $8,000 paid to the qualified advisor.

John decides to get started. I'm John's advisor. John says he wants to get started at the bottom and work his way up. Now there isn't anything wrong with that if that's all you can do. So I tell John that he should expect to see several thousand dollars go right through his hands into mine. I tell him this so he doesn't come back and say I didn't tell him about positioning. John and I work together to get his training sales knocked out and by the second week, John is qualified and in a money-earning position. The second week John has three guests at the presentation. When the presentation is over and all the questions are answered, two of the three decide to get started. This is great for John, because he is qualified and is about to make money.

Well, the two guests who are going to get started are coming in at the top. They are buying all the products at once because they see that it's the smartest business decision. John is about to make the $1,000 commission on each of the two sales, but since John is not qualified at the top, I make $13,000 from each one of John's guests. That's $26,000 that should have gone to John but went to me instead, because John didn't position himself. That can sting a little, and generally it only takes this happening once before John decides to go ahead and position himself.

It's important to realize that you as the associate are going to spend the same amount of money to get positioned whether you do it now or later. The difference in the Australian two-up compensation plan is how much income you will pass up while you are waiting to get positioned at the top. Income that should and could go to you will go to your advisor through no effort of his or her own.

Check with your advisor or your company to verify the type of compensation plan that is in place and how to take advantage of positioning so that you can maximize your earning potential. The difference for you in your first year could be six figures just by itself. You don't want to lose income that could be yours.

FLIGHT PLAN DESTINATION

As I bring this book to a close, I would like to go back to the flight plan we filed in Chapter One. I stated that if you intend to get where you are going, you must know where you are presently, what I referred to as the departure point. I trust that if you have made it to this point in the book, you have not only found your departure point, you have also realized your destination as well as your route of flight, meaning where you are going and how you will get there. If this is the case, then you have successfully filed and completed your flight plan.

By utilizing the information in this book and continuing to expect success in all that you do with your business and your life, you will inspire others to achieve more and greater levels of success. The more your business grows, the more the tips and techniques contained in this book will play a part in your success, so make sure you review the chapters in this book often. I encourage you to continue to focus on your goals as well as continuing to help others reach their own goals. If you concentrate on helping others as you build your own business, the universe will reward you with the manifestation of your goals and dreams.

With that, I would like to welcome you to your flight plan destination, your new result. Whether this is your first day in a network marketing business or you are a seasoned veteran, by practicing the techniques I have outlined, you will be able to reprogram your own auto pilot to fly directly to the new destination called success. Congratulations.

CHAPTER **8** SUMMARY

*I*f your company has different options for getting started, chances are good that the highest starting position is going to require that you spend a little more money on your business than if you started at the lowest level. This may require that you purchase a certain product or an amount of product in order to do so. It may require that you commit to a certain amount or level of work or service. Either way, you are the one who determines how fast you will start generating income and how much income you will generate. If given a choice, do you want to make a lot or a little? Do you want to make it fast or slow? Positioning gives you the ability to choose.

I suggest looking at it like a business owner and realizing that the total amount to get started at the highest point of almost any company is still far less than the capital outlay for most conventional businesses and franchises.

In short, positioning is absolutely key to the amount of time it takes you to have success in your business. Speaking from experience, I can tell you that not positioning yourself as quickly as you possibly can can cost you thousands and thousands of dollars. As a new associate with a network marketing company, it is important to look at the positioning options when you first enroll with the company. Waiting to get positioned could be the difference between being a top income earner and just an associate.

The Key

The last thing I would like to leave you with is what I call "the key." In short, if you truly want to make a multiple six- or seven-figure income, the key is to forget about your income and concentrate on helping your associates and even people who are not financially connected to you make money and become successful.

The laws of the universe of abundance say that what you put out will come back to you tenfold. Don't worry about your income. If you are helping others become successful and practicing the techniques I've outlined in this book, you will make plenty of money. *This business is about helping other people improve the quality of their lives. Do not forget that, and never quit!*

With that, I would like to congratulate you on your new success, and I look forward to meeting you at an event in the future!

Appendix A

Goal Contract*

BINDING CONTRACT OF COMMITMENT

Name: _____ Date _____

It is the intention of the undersigned to move toward this goal in thought and action and to make all of the positive choices necessary to obtain it.

I understand that this goal is what I want for me and that every positive choice I make, no matter how small, is a step toward the fulfillment of this goal. From this day forward I will not be denied any longer. This is the day in my life that I finally make the choices that I need to and quit taking the easy way out. I will pay the price that is necessary to reach my goal, because I know the pain of not fulfilling myself is greater than the pain of doing any job, no matter how difficult.

_____

_____

_____

_____

_____

_____

_____

_____

_____

_____
Signature of Intent

INTENTION FULFILLED

Congratulations! You created a vision in your mind and brought that vision into reality in your life by believing in that vision and moving relentlessly toward it through wise choices.

_____   _____
Date Fulfilled   Signature of Acceptance

From Premeditated Success by Tom Murphy

Appendix B

Goal Contract Terms and Conditions*

1. Write out a vivid description of your goal, along with your name and starting date.
2. Your written goal should be very descriptive and explicit. Use all of your senses so that you can paint a very clear picture of what is wanted and when.
3. Your goal should be something that you want badly enough to turn you on and make you move and act with enthusiasm.
4. Use this contract with yourself *for any* goal, no matter how small or large. A goal, no matter its size, should be treated with respect, because it builds your character and self-image.
5. Put the power of choice to work for you. All choices you make will move you away from or toward your goal. Always be aware of these choices and take the upward path toward your dreams.
6. Remember, you can be as great as anyone, but you must have a written plan. Each of these goals and choices, no matter how small, will become part of the plan and turn your beautiful dreams into a fantastic and rewarding life.
7. All of your letters of intent that have not been completed should be read and visualized every day with great conviction, so as to imbed your goals in your subconscious mind.
8. If you want your life to change, you have to change or you are going to stay just about the same as you are now. So set goals that turn you on and get your life into gear. You can do it; you can change and become or do anything you want.
9. What you are doing here is deadly serious. You cannot reach the place you desire if you do not know how to get there. It's the same way for life. Each one of your goals becomes a stopping point or a starting point on the road map of your life. These goals will become a guide for your every success. If you don't have a map, how are you going to stay on course towards your dreams?
10. When a goal is reached, sign off and then write in large letters on the face of the letter of intent, "This contract is fulfilled." Save all of these letters of intent and keep them in order by date completed. They will become an autobiography of your success and growth. You will be able to draw great strength from this string of successes that you have accomplished, no matter how small or how hard they may seem at first. Be grateful for all that you have and the power that you have to create a better life every day.

*From Premeditated Success *by Tom Murphy*

Appendix C

Goal Call-Back Script

Good evening, may I speak to _____? Hi _____ , this is _____ . I'm calling in regard to a _____ that you responded to requesting some information about working from your home. Have I caught you at a good time? Great. _____ I take it since you responded to the _____ , you must be pretty serious about finding a business of your own; is that right? Good. Well, let me tell you a little about what I do. First of all, I work with a company that is based in _____ called _____ . Are you familiar with us? Okay.

Well, what I do is speak to people just like you who are looking for a way to increase their income working from home. I'm going to tell you right now, I'm looking for some very serious people. I'm talking about people who want to earn no less than six figures in the next six to twelve months. So I sort right through most of the people I talk to because, quite frankly, not everybody believes that's possible. So what I would like to do right now is ask you a couple of quick questions to find out exactly what you're looking for. That way I know I'm not going to waste your time or mine. Fair enough? Great.

■ What do you do for a living right now? How long? How's it going? (Write down the answers.)

- What's the main reason you're looking for a business of your own?

- What level of income are you accustomed to right now?

- More importantly, _____ , ideally, what kind of income would you like to be generating on a monthly basis?

- Given that this is a business, there will be some start-up costs. If I can show you without a doubt how you can generate six figures in the next six to twelve months, are you in a position where you could come up with about $_____ to get your business off the ground?

Well, _____ , I can definitely tell you that earning $_____ in the next twelve months with this company is very attainable, and the reason is that we have a system in place that virtually anyone can duplicate. As long as they're coachable and trainable and they don't try to reinvent the wheel, anyone can do this and have success. So, what I would suggest is, *if you're very serious* about earning that hundred or two hundred thousand dollars in the next twelve months, that you and I get together as soon as possible so you can take a look at this business and get all your questions answered and see if this is something that is a match for you.

The best way to do that is for you to attend my business presentation on _____ evening at _____ , if that would work for your schedule. Great. Let me get you some directions. (Email or fax the directions immediately if possible.)

Now, _____ , this is what I would ask of you: if for any reason you have a problem and you can't make it, I ask that you give me a courtesy call to let me know. Here's the way I work. If you don't show and you don't call, I will not waste my time calling you back. Fair enough? Great. _____ , I enjoyed talking with you and I'll look forward to meeting you on _____ evening. See you then.

Appendix D

Prospecting Call FAQ'S

I don't remember responding to any ad . . .

- That's okay, but are you seriously looking for a business of your own?
- *Well, that's really not important, but are you looking for a business of your own?*

Well, what's this all about?

- This is about you making a ton of money working from your home . . . How serious are you?
- *This is about me seeing if you qualify for my time . . . Are you coachable and trainable?*

Well, what are you sellin?

- I'm not selling anything . . . we've got a system that takes care of that.
- You know, the great part about this business is I don't have to do any selling or explaining . . . and of course neither would you.
- *Of course we've got products, but I don't do any personal selling whatsoever.*

How much does it cost . . . ?

- It doesn't cost a thing to get the information.
- *That's totally up to you . . . it would be your own business; you can set it up how you want.*

Is this going to cost me anything?

- *Of course. This is a legitimate business; you can't start a business for free . . . could you could start a McDonald's for free?*

Is this a pyramid?

- Absolutely not.
- *Absolutely . . . (click; hang up)*

Well, can't you tell me a little bit about it? I'm not going to come down if I don't know what it is.

- Sure, I could sit here for the next two hours trying to explain this business to you and chances are you would still not be clear. See, the great thing about this business is I don't have to do any selling or explaining and of course neither would you. My job is simply to see if you qualify for my time because, again, I'm looking for serious people . . . Now, how serious are you, cause if you're not serious I'm going to go ahead and let you go.

- I could, but I'm not going to because it would take too long and you wouldn't be clear on everything. The reason we do the business presentation is that, quite frankly, that's the most effective way to get you all the information and get your questions answered so that you can make an intelligent decision on whether this is something that's a match for you or not.

- No . . . that's not my job. It's my job to find out whether you're the type of person I would like to work with. If you're serious about making that multiple six-figure income, then I would suggest you come and sit down with me on Thursday and get all your questions answered.

■ Let me get this straight . . . you just told me that you want to make $200,000 in the next year and I'm offering you an opportunity that will allow you to do just that and you're not willing to take a look at it? Just how serious are you? . . . Cause if you're not serious, I'm going to let you go.

(If someone keeps interrupting you with questions)

■ Wait a minute . . . let's back up here. You answered my ad. I'm the one with the opportunity here and I'm looking for people who are coachable and trainable. Right now it would not appear that you are coachable or trainable. So if you're serious, we can go forward; but if you're not, I'm going to let you go.

■ *You know, John, I don't think this is going to be for you, so I'm going to let you go. Have a great night."* *(Click)*

How much will I have to work?

■ *The beauty of this business is that you can work as little or as much as you want. You are working for yourself.*

How much money have you made?

■ *The real question is not how much money I've made, but how much money are you going to make?*

How long have you been in the business?

■ Are you talking about myself personally or the company? Me, I've been in this business for

several months. _____ is a company that
has been in business since _____ .
Tell me, _____ , when do you want to start
making money?

Do you have any other questions about making money?

Can't you send something in the mail?

I don't do mailings. That is why we have business presentations. When you are serious, not just curious about changing the quality of your life, give me a call.

FREE STUFF

Share this book with two friends who purchase the book
and you will also receive:

- A **<u>FREE</u>** thirty-minute personal coaching session certificate
- **<u>FREE</u>** admission to one of my live events anytime in the next twelve months
- **<u>50% off</u>** the audio version of this book (CD only)

To take advantage of this offer:

Write your name on the two coupons below, cut them out, and share them with two fellow marketers. Have them call

1-800-247-6553

and mention the name on the coupon when they order their copy. It's that easy.

To order your copy of

How I Made Six Figures in ONE Month

call **1-800-247-6533**

and tell the operator that the person listed below referred you.

Thank you for your order.

_____

(Referring name goes here)

To order your copy of

How I Made Six Figures in ONE Month

call **1-800-247-6533**

and tell the operator that the person listed below referred you.

Thank you for your order.

_____

(Referring name goes here)